W9-CPF-127

THOMAS COOK
Travellers

PROVENCE

BY
ROGER THOMAS

Produced by AA Publishing

Written by Roger Thomas

Original photography by Adrian Baker

Edited, designed and produced by AA Publishing.
© The Automobile Association 1995.
Maps © The Automobile Association 1995.

A CIP catalogue record for this book is available from the British Library.

ISBN 0 7495 0958 9

The contents of this publication are believed correct at the time of printing. Nevertheless, the publishers cannot accept responsibility for any errors or omissions, or for changes in the details given in this guide, or for the consequences of any reliance on the information provided by the same. Assessments of attractions, hotels, restaurants and so forth are based upon the author's own experience, and therefore descriptions given in this guide necessarily contain an element of subjective opinion which may not reflect the publisher's opinion or dictate a reader's own experiences on another occasion.
We have tried to ensure accuracy in this guide, but things do change and we would be grateful if readers would advise us of any inaccuracies they may encounter.

Published by AA Publishing (a trading name of Automobile Association Developments Limited, whose registered office is Norfolk House, Priestley Road, Basingstoke, Hampshire RG24 9NY. Registered number 1878835) and the Thomas Cook Group Ltd.

Colour separation: BTB Colour Reproduction, Whitchurch, Hampshire.

Printed by Edicoes ASA, Oporto, Portugal.

Cover picture: *Pont du Gard*
Title page: *Arles*
Above: *sun-baked corner of Roussillon*

Contents

About this Book

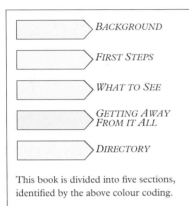

> BACKGROUND
>
> FIRST STEPS
>
> WHAT TO SEE
>
> GETTING AWAY FROM IT ALL
>
> DIRECTORY

This book is divided into five sections, identified by the above colour coding.

The spirit of Van Gogh and Cézanne lives on in Provence, still a mecca for artists

Background gives an introduction to the region – its history, geography, politics, culture.
First Steps offers practical advice on arriving and getting around.
What to See is an alphabetical listing of places to visit, interspersed with walks and tours.
Getting Away From it All highlights places off the beaten track where it's possible to enjoy peace and quiet.
Finally, the **Directory** provides practical information – from shopping and entertainment to children and sport, including a section on business matters. Special highly illustrated features on specific aspects of the region appear throughout the book.

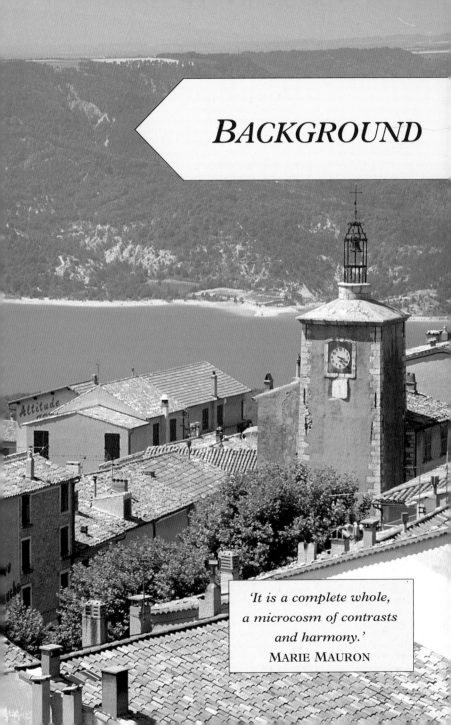

BACKGROUND

'It is a complete whole,
a microcosm of contrasts
and harmony.'
MARIE MAURON

Introduction

*P*rovence is undoubtedly the most alluring part of France. It is also perhaps the most complex. The phrase 'land of contrasts' crops up with disturbing – and unjustifiable – regularity in many guidebooks. In the case of this particular one, it is unavoidable. Provence displays at least two incompatible personality traits. There is the pastoral face of Provence, a seductive visage of sleepy, golden-stoned farmhouses, sunflowers, lavender fields, vineyards, olive groves and improbably blue skies. Clashing with this bucolic vision is the Provence of the coast, a cosmopolitan – and often chaotic – mix of glamorous resorts and dense development, a victory of style over simplicity, conspicuous consumption over quiet contemplation.

LOCATOR

Belt industries of this blessed, beautiful, blighted 'California of Europe'.

Provence can give you whatever you want. A hundred kilometres from the coast, you can sit in a café in a fountained medieval square and watch the world go by – which will probably consist of one man and his bicycle or *madame* doing the shopping. An hour's drive away, you can rub shoulders with the seriously rich and famous on a jewelled coastal strip that is still *the* place to go and be seen, that still has the *cachet*, that still attracts yachts worth more than the Gross Domestic Product of many Third World countries.

Further adding to the complex character of the area are its Alpine regions, where snow-capped peaks reach up into sunny skies; its high, empty plateaux, a no-man's-land between the Mediterranean and the Alps; its deep gorges like giant incisions in the Earth's crust; its vast, lagoon-like flatlands along the Rhône delta; its retrospective qualities, embodied by an outstanding Roman heritage and idyllic medieval towns; and its dynamic, ever-onward economic impetus, driven by the high-tech Sun

THOMAS COOK'S PROVENCE

In 1871 Thomas Cook advertised the new destinations of Menton, Nice, Toulon and Marseille as part of the 'Winter Arrangements' for that year. By the 1880s, Cook's Christmas and New Year trips to the South of France were very popular with his middle- and upper-class customers.

A scene of order and plenty: farmhouse and vineyard near Ménerbes in the Lubéron

PROVENCE

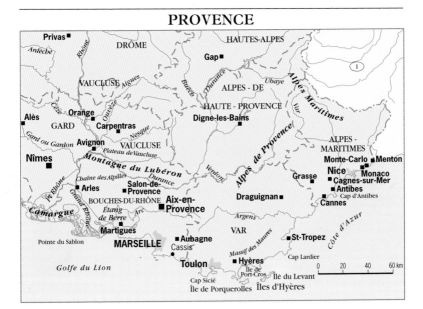

History

Mesolithic times (Middle Stone Age)
Earliest known inhabitants.
6000BC
Evidence of Neolithic (New Stone Age) pottery and agriculture.
around 600BC
Greek colonists found *Massalia* (Marseille).
600–100BC
Further Greek settlement along the coast, leading to clashes with the native population. Greeks enlist the aid of their Roman allies.
150–50BC
Romans advance into Provence.
58–52BC
Conquest of Gaul by Julius Caesar.
46BC
Roman amphitheatre is built at Arles.
19BC
Construction of the Pont du Gard aqueduct near Nîmes.
1st century AD
Roman conquest of Provence completed early in the century.

Julius Caesar gazes down from a wall in Arles

2nd–3rd centuries AD
Roman influence at its height: roads constructed, new towns founded, trade increased.
4th–5th centuries AD
Christianity gains in importance.
471
Arles invaded and taken by Visigoths, a western Germanic people.
476
Fall of the Roman Empire. Within 50 years, Provence is taken over by the Franks, another western Germanic people.
736–739
Saracens, nomadic Arabs from the deserts of Africa and the Middle East, invade southern France.
768–814
Charlemagne becomes king of the Francs and brings a semblance of order to Provence.
855
Provence is made a kingdom.
9th century
Continuing incursions by the Saracens.
1032
Provence becomes part of the Holy Roman Empire, though the Counts of Provence retain their independence.
12th century
The Crusades lead to increasing prosperity along the coast.
12th–14th centuries
The era of the troubadours, poet-musicians whose major theme was courtly love.
1274
The papacy is given land – known as the Comtat Venaissin – in Provence. This influential episode paves the way for further papal links.

1309
The French Pope Clement V escapes political interferences in faction-ridden Rome by setting up court in Avignon.

1378–1417
The Great Schism of the Church, with one pope in Rome and the other in Avignon.

1409
The university at Aix-en-Provence is established.

1434–80
Provence flourishes under René of Anjou (Good King René).

c1480
Provence becomes part of France.

1486
The union of Provence with the crown is ratified at Aix-en-Provence.

1545
Religious massacre in the Lubéron Hills. Catholics and Protestants become embroiled in the Wars of Religion (1562–98).

1555
Nostradamus, physician and astrologer, publishes his predictions.

1580–95
Marseille becomes an important trading centre.

1629
Provence is affected by the Plague.

1720–22
The region is devastated by a terrible epidemic of the Plague, killing 100,000 in two years.

1789–99
The French Revolution.

1792
In support of the revolutionary cause, 500 volunteers from Marseille parade in Paris to the *Song of the Rhine Army*. The song is rechristened *La Marseillaise* and becomes the French national anthem.

1793
The Siege of Toulon, during which the young Napoléon Bonaparte makes his mark.

1804
Napoléon crowns himself emperor and proceeds to conquer much of Europe.

1813
After conflict with Britain and neighbouring Continental countries, Europe rises against Napoléon. His massive defeat at Leipzig forces his abdication and exile to island of Elba.

1815
Napoléon returns from exile to his short-lived 'Hundred Days' of power, but is defeated at the Battle of Waterloo. His second exile is on the island of St Helena.

1860s
Casinos open at Monte-Carlo.

1914–18
World War I does not affect Provence territorially, though many of its men are killed in service.

1939–45
The Italians occupy Menton in 1940, followed by large-scale German occupation in 1942, during which the French scuttle their fleet at Toulon. Allied troops land on the Côte d'Azur in 1944. Germans remain in the mountains until 1945.

1945
Col de Tende is ceded from Italy to France.

1962
Airport opens at Nice and soon becomes an international hub.

1970
Autoroute opens between Paris and Marseille.

1981
The high-speed TGV train links Paris with Marseille.

Geography

*P*rovence's boundaries embrace an amazing variety of scenery. Fertile valleys rise into rugged mountains, wooded hillsides and richly cultivated plains drift down to a palm-fringed, sandy coast. Towering crags and deep gorges in the Alpine country to the northeast contrast with the marshlands and long beaches of the Rhône delta to the southwest.

River and road

The fast-flowing Rhône has played a vital role in the development of trade. As well as defining Provence's western boundary, its broad valley is the region's crucial communications artery with the north, carrying the main road and rail links. Provence's other major river, the Durance, runs east to west, flowing into the Rhône south of Avignon.

Upland Provence

The mountain ranges striding across

The Grand Cañon du Verdon, almost 1,000m deep and an awe-inspiring sight

Provence are part of the geological upheaval that, over vast stretches of time, created the Alps. Mont Ventoux, the towering 1,909m guardian of the northwestern approach to the region, has an overwhelming presence set off by vine-clad foothills. The northeastern gateway to Provence is through the mountains of the Alpes-de-Hautes-Provence, a highland area unremittingly Alpine in character.

South-central Provence also has its uplands. The Lubéron Mountains, although only half the height of Ventoux, are nonetheless a prominent upland barrier between the Plateau de Vaucluse

and the coast. Winter sunshine along the Riviera highlights the proximity of the snowy peaks of the Alpes-Maritimes, only a short distance inland. You are never far away from hills and mountains in Provence: even the flat Rhône delta suddenly rises into the craggy Alpilles, a western offshoot of the Lubéron range.

Gorges and sunken valleys

The limestone rocks of this region result in weirdly eroded mountain features (the Vaucluse's Dentelles de Montmirail are a classic – see page 33). The rock also produces a near-subterranean spectacle where the limestone massifs have been intercut with deep gorges by the patient action of rivers. The most spectacular is the Grand Cañon du Verdon (see pages 130–1), where the river snakes between cliffs almost 1km high. Along the coast west of Marseille, limestone valleys have sunk into the sea to produce a strange, fjord-like shoreline of deeply indented inlets known as _calanques_ (see page 63).

Climate

Generally speaking, Provence is a region of hot, dry summers and mild, sunny winters: a climate that continues to entice the pleasure seekers as well as immigrants (usually from the grey northern latitudes) attracted as much by Provence's sunshine record as its new industries. An exception to this general rule can be made for the more northerly mountainous areas, which are cooler and wetter in spring and autumn but provide ideal conditions for winter sports. Western parts of Provence are regularly exposed to the _mistral_, a penetrating north wind (see pages 12–13).

The hottest months are July and August, when temperatures soar to around 28°C and rainfall is minimal.

Vertiginous Gourdon, perched above the River Loup, 14km northeast of Grasse

Some visitors prefer Provence in the spring, when the air is pleasantly warm and the countryside full of fresh, bright colours. Winters in the coastal region are mild, but autumn produces rainy weather in October and November.

Economy

Agriculture remains an important part of the economy. Once-arid regions have long served as productive farmland thanks to centuries of irrigation, and Provence continues to produce more fruit and vegetables than any other part of France. Honey, herbs and fields of lavender are much in evidence. Perfume, oils and soaps, textiles, crystallised fruit, mines and salt beds reflect some of the traditional Provençal occupations. There is a significant wine industry, based mainly on the Côtes du Rhône _appellation_. Much of Provence's industry is also concentrated in the Rhône Valley, and in recent years high-tech, scientific and communications industries have expanded considerably. The port of Marseille – one of the largest cities in France – is a busy commercial centre.

THE *MISTRAL*

The *mistral* has been known to drive man and beast mad. Suicide and murder rates are said to increase when this violent wind whistles down the Rhône Valley, blowing with sustained intensity for days on end (it can last for anything from three to 10 days). Its name derives from the Provençal *mistrau*, meaning master. The wind, which can reach speeds of 200km/h, has undoubtedly tamed those unfortunate enough to live in its direct path. While in other countries the weather provokes comment of a general nature, in Provence the *mistral* has inspired all kinds of theories and speculations about the onset and duration of this unwelcome visitor.

When pressure is high over the mountains or low over the sea, the wind sweeps down from the Massif Central to the Mediterranean, gaining in force as it funnels through the Rhône Valley. If it blows in summer, this cold wind will soon have you reaching for a sweater, even on the sunniest day. When it blows in winter, the chill factor seems positively Siberian – which explains why all wise Provençals have windowless north-facing walls, not to mention hefty stones to hold down the tiles on their roofs, as protection against this insidious, insistent enemy. Provence's decorative wrought-iron bell towers – known as *campaniles* – are another testament to the power of the *mistral*: the wind rushes harmlessly through the ironwork cage instead of toppling a conventional stone spire.

The wind is not entirely a dark force. It clears the sky of clouds, leaving a post-*mistral* blue of wondrous intensity. Farmers sometimes refer to it as *mange fange* (mud eater), because it dries up the mud. It mainly affects the Rhône Valley and its hinterland, rarely extending further east than Toulon.

Do not, for one moment, think that the many *'Mistral'* references you will see in street names are in honour of the wind. The Provençals are remembering their celebrated poet, cultural historian and man of letters Frédéric Mistral (1830–1914), not the eponymous enemy.

An ironwork bell cage in Ménerbes offers no resistance to the rage of the *mistral*

Winter or summer, the *mistral* can sweep across the Provençal countryside turning paradise into hell

Culture

*T*he culture of Provence finds expression everywhere: not just in artistic events, but in the way people live and in the traditions they have inherited from their forebears. In ancient times the region was a staging post between the Mediterranean in the south and Gaul to the north. The resulting cross-fertilisation of cultures has produced a unique mix.

Generalisation is a notorious activity. There will always be those who claim that the worldly inhabitants of Aix or Avignon harbour pretensions of sophistication unknown to the humble Provençal peasant (if such a species exists any longer). Nonetheless, it is reasonable to claim that Provençals are a proud and independent people who, though wary and to some degree suspicious of strangers, can be hospitable and generous to a fault once their trust has been earned. They have a dialect of their own, Provençal, which although not commonly spoken today is still taught as an option in most schools. It differs in many respects from classical French and is distinguished by the richness of its vowels (see page 22).

Festivals and *fêtes*

The pastoral tradition remains strong in Provence. The French in general have an almost mystical relationship with the land. Many city dwellers are today's representatives of families who, until relatively recently, lived a rural existence.

The people of Provence have a strong sense of their heritage and like to keep traditions alive

Fruits of the earth at a village fête

the finest to be seen anywhere, and richly decorated medieval churches demonstrate the degree of spiritual and material wealth the people have invested in their religious life. Romanesque chapels and wayside shrines add to the region's diversity. Among Provence's most distinctive features are the dry-stone beehive huts known as *bories*, originally the work of semi-nomadic shepherds; the best examples are in the Lubéron.

Although the most modern of industries are nowadays to be found in Provence, the locals pride themselves on their deep attachment to the land. For them it is also a matter of continuity, seen in their reverence for traditions, many of which are rooted in rural antiquity.

Some of the festivals and *fêtes* with which the region abounds celebrate the harvesting of crops and the generosity of nature. Flower parades and wine festivals add zest and colour to the life of many a town and village, special events mark the custom of transhumance (the migration of sheep from winter plain to summer pasture), while fishermen's festivals are evidence of the importance of the sea. Adept though the early Christians were at giving new meaning to old customs, distinctly pagan undertones linger on in some of these local festivals.

Rural festivals flourish alongside more sophisticated occasions such as the Cannes Film Festival (see pages 98–9) and musical events of various kinds. Sophisticates can enjoy everything from opera to jazz, for instance, at summer festivals in Arles and Avignon.

Architecture

Visitors with an eye for architecture will find much to delight them in Provence. The region's Roman remains are among

Bee-hive-like *bories* near Gordes

Crafts old and new

The earliest inhabitants of Provence, although belonging to a hunting and fishing culture, were by no means savages. The necklaces of fishbone found on prehistoric skeletons uncovered here prove their manual dexterity and aesthetic sense.

Artistry of a different kind flourishes in Provence today, a region famous for the quality of its craftwork. From the religious figurines known as *santons* (see page 125) to the blown-glass bubbles of Biot, Provence has a wealth of beautiful objects to tempt the discriminating visitor. It is not difficult to discern a continuity at work here, typified by the way old blends with new in this heritage-conscious part of France.

Politics

*P*rovence was once a kingdom on its own, though it officially became a part of France in 1486. Union with France did not have much influence on the way of life because of the great distances from Paris, reinforced by Provence's ancient ties with Italy. But everything was to change with the coming of the railways in the second half of the 19th century. Not only was the local Provençal language undermined by French, but the region attracted tourists and winter residents who created along the coast a cosmopolitan and wealthy society far removed in its values and lifestyle from the traditional countryfolk of the region.

This pattern produced the extremes of right-wing power in cities such as Nice and Cannes, and socialist or communist strongholds inland. But even among the cities, there are exceptions to the rule. The biggest city in Provence is Marseille. It has for many years been socialist (notwithstanding a worrying far-right enclave) with a suspicion of central government. Nice, on the other hand, has an unequivocally right-wing tradition. A single family ruled that city for many decades, and its reign ended only when the mayor, accused of large-scale corruption, fled to South America.

Since Algeria gained independence from France in the late 1950s, Provence has become home for hundreds of thousands of *pieds noirs*, the French settlers who fled back to the mother country. They have constituted a defined political force, and it seems probable that the presence of this uprooted and vengeful community has accounted for the high level of support for the National Front in cities such as Toulon and Nice and in smaller places like Aubagne. Right-wing opinion is fuelled by what is perceived as a problem with North African immigrants and other 'foreigners'. In the 1980s Jean-Marie Le Pen's National Front party started to gain a foothold in the south. Le Pen stood unsuccessfully as a candidate in Nice in the 1993 general election.

Provence forms part of the Provence-Alpes-Côte d'Azur regional government, which is controlled by the right.

Once a separate kingdom, Provence came under the French flag in 1486

One of the greatest blows to Provençal cultural autonomy was the edict of Villers-Coterets, in 1539, which decreed French would be the official language in schools, churches and the administration

FIRST STEPS

'Most people come here for the light
and the picturesque quality. As for me,
I come from the north. What made me stay
are the great coloured reflections of
January, the luminosity of daylight.'
HENRI MATISSE
1869–1954

First Steps

*P*rovence is a fairly complicated jigsaw puzzle. At the risk of stating the obvious, the basic advice for the first-time visitor is to do one of two things: head inland for the escapist rural retreat (found anywhere within 50km of the coast) or pack the swimsuits and the evening dress for the beaches and casinos.

Some prefer the lush vineyards of the Vaucluse, others the more barren high country of the Var or the mountains of the Alpes-de-Haute-Provence. The glamour and glitz of Cannes and St-Tropez cast an irresistible spell over many, while others prefer the uncomplicated appeal of family resorts such as La Ciotat or the natural wonders of the Camargue.

Finding your way around

This book is subdivided into the region's five *départements* – Vaucluse, Bouches-du-Rhône, Var, Alpes-Maritimes and Alpes-de-Haute-Provence. If each *département* were a self-contained entity with its own unique, distinct set of scenic characteristics, then the task of explaining 'what is where' in Provence would be a simple one. But Provence is not that tidily arranged. The classic violator of departmental borders is the Côte d'Azur, the 'azure-blue coastline'. We have all heard of it, but where exactly is it? Theoretically it stretches from St-Raphaël (in the Var), along the coast of the Alpes-Maritimes, through the independent Principality of Monaco to the Italian border. In practice, the Côte d'Azur label is often applied to the entire French Riviera as far west as Cassis (in the Bouches-du-Rhône).

Similarly, major landscape features such as the Montagne du Lubéron and the Alpine Parc National du Mercantour span departmental boundaries. Overlap also applies to the precise definition of Provence itself. Within the context of this book, Nîmes, Pont du Gard and the western Camargue are all included within the Bouches-du-Rhône section, even though this is not strictly correct (these places are in the *département* of the Gard).

Cities and coastal resorts

Provence, for all its natural beauty, also boasts big cities and busy resorts. The

---

PERCHED VILLAGES

'A village stands on high ground, partly as a defence against the Saracens, but mainly for the good view ... The peasants, who know how to enjoy life, take time to look at things.'

These were the words of Provençal writer Jean Giono (1895–1970). The 'perched villages' (*villages perchés*) of Provence were built for security in troubled medieval times, though few proved to be impregnable. By the start of this century, many were in a sorry state, the locals understandably preferring life in newer houses with running water and other conveniences. Nowadays the immaculately renovated villages – many with shops, artisans' quarters and exclusive restaurants – make every attempt to attract rather than repel visitors.

cities vary from stylish Aix to sprawling Marseille, slightly dowdy Arles to self-confident Avignon. The resorts, too, have distinct characters. A coastal strip that seems on first impressions to be a continuous, unbroken development reveals undeniable differences on closer examination.

The old maxim 'Cannes is for living, Monte-Carlo for gambling and Menton for dying' still has a ring of truth. Nice and St-Tropez, the other really famous places along the coast, have similarly strong – and surprising – personalities: surprising because of the vastness of Nice (which is more city than resort) and the smallness of world-famous St-Tropez.

Resorts such as Hyères and Ste-Maxime manage to preserve a sense of dignity on an intensely developed, over-exploited coast, which unfortunately shows all the signs of overheating (in the non-climatic sense). Yet there are still areas of relative wilderness: the indented coast between Marseille and Cassis, the lovely Îles d'Hyères and, to a lesser extent, the mountain-backed shorelines fringing the Massif des Maures and Massif de l'Esterel.

In the country
Provence's landscapes range from sunny valleys to snowy peaks. The characteristic Provençal scene – the golden-stoned farmhouse set amongst sun-baked vineyards – is most readily found in the Vaucluse or Bouches-du-Rhône. The higher country of the Vaucluse Plateau and the Var offers huge, open spaces that reveal a hint of Alpine influence. The Alps themselves lie further north and east, in the thinly populated upper reaches of the Alpes-de-Haute-Provence and the Alpes-Maritimes.

Villefranche-sur-Mer, one of the less frenetic resorts on the popular Côte d'Azur

Dressing up in local costume, singing and dancing are all part of the fun of a festival

Customs and lifestyle

Provence is a land where undue haste is not considered a virtue. Its people are far from indolent, but they instinctively believe that quality of life is much more important than intensity of activity. Even in the busiest cities such as Marseille, time is found for a leisurely lunch.

To understand the character of the Provençals, one must appreciate that from time immemorial their lives have been shaped by the slow turn of the seasons. They are essentially a rural people with respect for the land, and this respect applies even to city folk, whose gardens are often small islands of perfection. Their natural reserve quickly gives way to open-handed generosity when they feel you are to be trusted, and their laughter and high spirits are infectious.

A hint of formality

The sense of being part of an old civilisation where the values of yesteryear are not easily discarded is confirmed by the etiquette of the region. Women are still greeted in the customary way with two or three kisses on the cheek (amongst men, even close friends observe a quick handshake), but this does not imply any taking of liberties. Manners tend to be far more formal than in Britain, for example, and the tourist would be well advised to address people as *monsieur, madame* or *mademoiselle.*

It also pays to know a little French, for an attempt to speak the language, however imperfectly, is regarded as an act of courtesy to the host country. Remember, too, that people living in the Provençal countryside are much more conservative than city dwellers in their attitude to dress. Topless bathing is perfectly acceptable on the beaches, but walking around town in beachwear is not. It is also a breach of propriety to enter a church or cathedral while scantily dressed.

Traditional costume

Tradition plays a large part in the life of Provence. The traditional costumes worn by many families during the numerous festivals bring a distinctive feel to life in the region. Christmas and Easter have their own special rituals, which are still faithfully observed.

In day-to-day matters, too, old customs die hard. Shopping is less a chore than a social activity that gives savour to life. Open-air markets not only offer goods and produce of all kinds, they also bring a town or village together once a week. These markets serve as a natural interface between locals and visitors to the region. To outsiders, they reveal how carefully the Provençals select the items that make up their everyday meals. These are folk not easily fobbed off with anything less than the best, for it seems that nature has equipped them with antennae highly sensitive to the shoddy and second-rate, enabling them to maintain high standards in a rapidly changing world.

A social dimension to food

Food, of course, is more than mere sustenance to the Provençals. Their insistence on quality reflects an attitude to food – found throughout France, in fact – that has profound social, even artistic, dimensions.

Calorie-conscious tourists may view such delights with trepidation, deciding perhaps that some of the salads served as separate courses are meals in themselves. What they should not deny themselves is the experience, for in Provence meals are

> **OPENING TIMES**
> Most religious sites are open at all reasonable times, though sightseeing visits should always take place when church services are not being held. Other sites often close in winter or have very restricted opening hours. Even in summer, many (especially museums) are closed at some time during the week, normally on Monday or Tuesday. Specific details are given for each site mentioned; in general all main sites are freely accessible and open daily during the tourist season.

social occasions to be enjoyed to the full.

Café society also flourishes here, and not only among the wealthier classes. Enjoying a *pastis* or *café crème* after a wander round the market is something that practically everyone does on a regular basis. It is part of the unhurried *vie provençale* (Provençal way of life).

The flower market in Aix-en-Provence

Language

Provençals are justly proud of the fact that their language continues to exist despite all the pressures exerted by mass communications and the cultural dominance of French. The official language of the region is, of course, French, but Provençal – the tongue of the medieval troubadours – still survives. Not that you are likely to hear it being spoken in the streets. Provençal today lives on as a literary language studied at school or university, and also – more visibly – on bilingual place-name signs.

Provençal is derived from the vulgar Latin that entered the region with Roman colonisation. It is a dialect of the southern Languedoc (the *langue d'oc* as opposed to the *langue d'oïl* of northern France, *oc* and *oïl* meaning 'yes' in the south and north respectively). Its written form reaches back 10 centuries, for around the year 1000 Provençal became the language of courtly poetry. Although gradually superseded by French as a written language, it survived as a spoken tongue until relatively recent times.

Provençal differs from French in the openness of its vowels. In standard French, unstressed vowels tend to contract or to disappear altogether, but in Provençal they are distinctly voiced. This makes for a rounder, more musical language, which in many respects is closely related to Catalan.

Optional lessons

A new awareness of the language arose in the first half of the 19th century, when the poet Frédéric Mistral helped found the Félibrige movement, which aimed to restore the Provençal language and codify its spellings. But revival proved a

forlorn hope, and by the time Mistral received the Nobel Prize in 1904, Provençal had already given way to French as the tongue in everyday use.

Today the language is taught as an option in most schools, and there is a faculty in the Provençal language and literature at the University of Aix-en-Provence. Its official encouragement should ensure its survival. It would take a brave – or foolhardy – person today to echo the sentiments of 19th-century tourist Lady Hester Stanhope, who in 1846 dared to pronounce it 'a most disagreeable jargon'!

WHAT TO SEE

'It is to be tranquilly overwhelmed
to see the Mediterranean just
before dawn, stretching out
beneath your windows. There will
be the grey satin of the sea, the
mountains behind, the absolutely
convincing outline of Reinach's
Greek villa at the end of
Beaulieu Point. And the memory
of Greek gods ...'

FORD MADOX FORD
It Was the Nightingale, 1933

Vaucluse

*V*ineyards, lavender fields and craggy hills cover this *département*, a beautiful area that lies under the watchful gaze of Mont Ventoux. The Vaucluse's western boundary is defined by the wide valley of the Rhône. Eastwards, the rich Côtes-du-Rhône vineyards rise into a roller-coaster landscape of green hills and valleys spread beneath the bare-topped heights of Mont Ventoux.

APT

This town, which spreads itself out across a wide valley on the northern approach to the Lubéron Mountains, is more noteworthy for its location than its inherent charm. It is mostly famous for its associations with things edible.

Apt is synonymous with sweets, speciality chocolates and candied fruit. There are a number of manufacturers,

Fountain in Apt. The town was once a place of pilgrimage but is now associated with sweets

some of whom specialise in glacéed or crystallised fruits – cherries, plums, pears, apricots, pineapples, etc. Apt's mouthwatering confections are on sale at the Saturday market, along with a magnificent array of local produce. The market, in the rue des Marchands, is a social as well as a shopping experience. Cars are banned from the town centre to make way for stallholders, musicians, jugglers and craftspeople. Apt also has a smaller 'farmer's market' on Tuesday morning (May to November) at cours Lauze de Perret.

Although the approach to the town is shabby and undistinguished, there are interesting and attractive little corners to explore. But most visitors inevitably look further afield, for the town is an excellent base for exploring the Parc Naturel Régional du Lubéron (see pages 46–7).

Ancienne Cathédrale Ste-Anne

This building, dedicated to the mother of the Virgin Mary, dates from the 11th century, though there is evidence of an earlier religious settlement in its two ancient crypts (Romanesque and pre-Romanesque).
In the centre of town.

Maison des Pays du Lubéron (Lubéron Regional Natural Park Office)

The visitor centre, in an attractive 17th-century mansion, has a wide range of information on the park, including a palaeontology museum.

1 place Jean-Jaurès. Tel: 90.74.08.55. Open: Monday to Saturday 9am–noon, 2–6pm (7pm in summer). Closed: Sunday. Free.

Musée Archéologique

Exhibits cover prehistory, the Gallo-Roman period (Apt was a prosperous Roman colony), and ceramics from the 17th to 19th centuries.

Rue de l'Amphithéâtre. Tel: 90.74.00.34. Open: summer, 10am–noon, 2.30–5.30pm; winter, 2.30–4.30pm. Closed: Tuesday and Sunday. Admission charge.

The cathedral of St Anne, Apt. Legend has it that the remains of the Virgin's mother lie here

VAUCLUSE

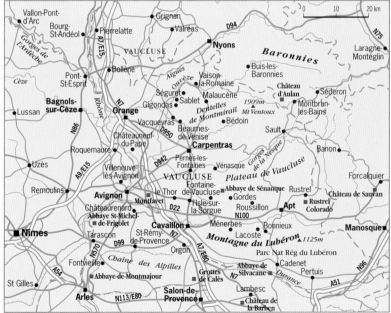

Avignon

*T*he historic, stylish city of Avignon stands alongside the curving Rhône on a wide, flat valley. It is the largest and most important city in the Vaucluse. Visitors approaching the city might begin to suspect that Avignon does not live up to expectations. Fear not: the historic heart of the city will not disappoint. Persevere through the bland suburbs to the ring of city walls, still complete, that enclose the Avignon of the guidebooks.

The walls, still defended by 39 towers, date from medieval times. Although Avignon's history can be traced as far back as the Bronze Age, its abiding personality was forged in the 14th century when it became the city of the Popes. In 1309 Pope Clement V sought refuge here from the factionalism of Rome, establishing an administrative base that eventually rivalled the Vatican. The imperial Palais des Papes (Palace of the Popes), still standing in its full glory, confirms Avignon's medieval status.

The city is today a major artistic centre. Its prestigious summer festival, focuses largely on the theatre and film. Across the river stands Avignon's sister city, Villeneuve-lès-Avignon. From the towers of Fort St-André there are stunning views looking back towards Avignon.

Cathédrale Notre-Dame-des-Doms

The magnificent tombs of two pontiffs can be seen within this 12th-century Romanesque church.
Place du Palais. Tel: 90.86.81.01.

Musée Calvet

This is Avignon's best museum. Dr Esprit Calvet bequeathed his collections to his native town. A fine 18th-century mansion contains classical and modern paintings, wrought-iron pieces, Greek scuplture and exhibits of local prehistory.

Rue Joseph Vernet. Tel: 90.86.33.84. Open: Wednesday to Monday 10am–noon, 2–6pm. Closed: Tuesday. Admission charge (free in winter).

Musée du Petit Palais

The museum, based at the episcopal palace acquired by the papacy in 1335, contains a huge collection of paintings and sculptures, mostly Italian of the 13th to 15th centuries.
Place du Palais. Tel: 90.86.44.58. Open: Wednesday to Monday summer, 9–11.50am, 2–6.15pm; winter, 9–11.50am, 2–6pm. Closed: Tuesday. Admission charge.

Musée Requien

Dedicated to Esprit Requien (1788–1851), the great Avignon naturalist, the museum has collections based on local botany, zoology and geology, a natural history library and a herbarium with over 200,000 specimens.
Rue Joseph Vernet, next to the Musée Calvet. Tel: 90.82.43.51. Open: Tuesday to Saturday 9am–noon, 2–6pm. Admission charge.

Palais des Papes

This majestic papal palace, with its dominant, soaring architecture, was built in the 14th century as a fortress-cum-palace to serve as a French base for the Popes. Its battlements and towers, reaching to 50m, are impressive enough.

Yet within the walls, the palace's overpowering dimensions are even more evident – especially the 48m-long Grand Tinel (Banqueting Hall) and Grande Audience (Great Audience Chamber). The palace is an overlap of two styles, reflecting the personalities of two Popes, Benoit XII and Clement VI. The first palace is sober, even austere, whereas the second is an opulent homage to an all-powerful prelate. During the French Revolution the Palais was ransacked and turned into first a prison, then a barracks, which it remained until early this century.
Place du Palais. Tel: 90.27.50.00 or 90.27.50.71. Open: mid-March to November, 9am–7pm (8pm in summer); November to mid-March, 9am–12.15pm, 2–6pm. Admission charge.

Pont St-Bénézet

This famous landmark is celebrated by the ubiquitous folk song *Sur le pont d'Avignon.* (The dancing mentioned in the song took place on an island in midstream, so technically the wording should be '*sous* [under] *le pont*' not '*sur* [on] *le pont*'.) The bridge itself comes as something of an anticlimax, for it no longer crosses the river. The stunted structure, once 900m long, was largely washed away in a 17th-century flood. Nevertheless, a walk along what is left of the narrow bridge is a ritual for all visitors to Avignon.
Tel: 90.85.60.16. Open: daily Easter to October, 10am–1pm, 2–6pm; November to Easter, 10am–noon, 1–5pm. Admission charge.

AVIGNON

THE POPES

Top: Clement V; Left: Clement VII

beatified, but Benoit XII was regarded as uncharitable and avaricious, and Clement VI – of noble birth and with tastes to match – continued his love affair, ennobled his 'nephew' and built a sumptuous 'new' palace reflecting his enthusiasm for the arts and high living. He also bought the city of Avignon (in return for absolution for the sin of complicity in the murder of the owner's first husband) for 80,000 florins, a sum only five times the cost of his inaugural banquet.

THE GREAT SCHISM

In 1377 Pope Gregory XI, a Frenchman, was persuaded to move the Holy See back to Rome and try to restore order to the warring states. But the Italian Urban VI, who soon followed him in 1378, upset the cardinals of France so much that they left Rome and elected a new French Pope in his place, Clement VII, recognised by the King of France. Thus the Great Schism of 1378–1417 was born, with one Pope in Rome and another in France. Christendom was split in two, both geographically and politically, with the 'Clementines' drawn up against the 'Urbanists'. They excommunicated each other and issued bulls calling for crusades against each other. The death of one or other of the Popes gave rise to fresh elections.

The two papacies were joined by a third in 1409, created by cardinals of the two parties hoping to find a compromise. Finally the crisis was resolved through a Church Council, at which a new Pope

Provence played a notable part in the convoluted religious life of the Middle Ages, for in the 14th century it became the seat of the papacy. This curious chapter in the history of Provence began in 1309 with the decision of Pope Clement V, who was French by birth, to set up court in a Dominican monastery in Avignon (he had never actually reached Rome since his election in 1305). He thus began what was unflatteringly described as 'the second Babylonian captivity of the Church', a period of preoccupation with power, legalism and money-raising.

The Popes who followed his lead were a mixed bunch: Urban V was later

The Avignon papal palace is a symbol of worldy wealth

Avignon was governed by a succession of papal legates. It remained papal property until the French Revolution.

was elected following the abdication or deposition of the other three.

Meanwhile, Avignon appears to have become exhausted by the controversy long before the Schism was resolved, for in 1403 the last of the Antipopes, Benoit XIII, was smuggled out of the Palais by a secret passage after a five-year siege by French troops, and the city settled into a more tranquil life. Even after the Schism, however,

Mont Ventoux provides the backdrop to the beautifully situated village of Bédoin

BEAUMES-DE-VENISE

This large village is known to many through its famous Muscat de Beaumes-de-Venise, a distinctive sweet amber-coloured wine. The village stands at the southern approach to the rugged Dentelles de Montmirail (see page 33), about 10km north of Carpentras. Narrow terraced streets climb into the hillside from an attractive central square lined with cafés and shops.

One kilometre to the west is the Chapelle de Notre-Dame d'Aubune, dating from the 9th and 10th centuries and topped by a tall square Romanesque bell tower. According to legend, Frankish and Saracen forces clashed here in the 8th century.

Wine-lovers will need no introduction to the villages around Beaumes – Vacqueyras, Gigondas, Sablet, Rasteau, Cairanne – for this area on the flattish eastern flank of the Rhône Valley produces the premier Côtes-du-Rhône Villages, a robust, peppery red wine

of formidable strength.
Beaumes is 9km north of Carpentras.

BÉDOIN

In winter, Bédoin is a sleepy village. In summer, it is transformed into a busy holiday centre. Do not try to drive through Bédoin on Monday morning, when the main street becomes a marketplace packed with stallholders and milling crowds.

Bédoin's popularity rests on its location. It stands at an altitude of over 300m, surrounded by beautiful wooded hills on the southern slopes of Mont Ventoux 15km northeast of Carpentras. Campsites and holiday homes attract a cosmopolitan mix of visitors (the area is particularly popular with the Dutch). You can soak up the sunny atmosphere in one of the many cafés along Bédoin's long main street.

For the children, the village has an excellent municipal swimming pool. Historically, there is little evidence of

Bédoin's ancient roots (it was founded in the 8th century), though there are vestiges of the medieval ramparts in the streets leading up to the hilltop church.

CARPENTRAS

For visitors, interest in Carpentras lies within the historic heart of the town; this is encircled by a ring of main arteries that follow the line of medieval fortifications (demolished in the 19th century). Compact central Carpentras is easily explored on foot. The towering Porte d'Orange, the main gateway into the old town from the north, is a lone, splendid medieval survivor. From this 14th-century gateway, the rue d'Orange and rue de l'Evêché lead into the pedestrianised town centre, dominated by the Palais de Justice (Law Courts) and the Cathédrale St-Siffrein. Guided tours of the Palais de Justice – formerly the episcopal palace, dating from the 17th century – are available in summer (enquire at the Office de Tourisme, 170 allée Jean-Jaurès). The cathedral, which is of limited interest, was started in 1404 and completed in the 17th century.

It is worth searching for the Arc de Triomphe hidden behind the Palais de Justice. This decorated Roman arch was probably built at about the same time as the more famous monument at Orange (see pages 36–7).

One of the Vaucluse's main markets is held in Carpentras each Friday morning. Look out for the stalls selling *berlingots*, the special caramel sweets for which the town is famous.

Musée Comtadin-Duplessis

Downstairs, the Musée Comtadin contains a wide-ranging collection of regional artefacts, including weapons, *santons* and bells worn by cattle and sheep. The Musée Duplessis, upstairs, displays the work of 18th-century Carpentras painter Joseph-Siffrein Duplessis and others.
234 boulevard Albin-Durand. Tel: 90.63.04.92. Open: Wednesday to Monday 10am–noon, 2–6pm (until 4pm November to March). Admission charge.

Musée Lapidaire

Housed in the former Convent of the Visitation, which has remarkable polychromatic decorations of the late 17th century, the museum contains prehistoric and Gallo-Roman collections together with columns from the Cathédrale St-Siffrein's Romanesque cloisters.
Rue des Saintes-Maries. Tel: 90.63.04.92. Open: Wednesday to Monday 10am–noon, 2–6pm (until 4pm November to March). Closed: Tuesday. Admission charge.

The Roman Arc de Triomphe in Carpentras

CAVAILLON

Fruit and vegetable fields fill the flattish, well-irrigated countryside around Cavaillon. One product in particular – the melon – is the mainstay of the area's thriving market gardening economy. Unsurprisingly, the town is home to the second largest wholesale fruit and vegetable market in France.

For a panoramic view of the fertile Cavaillon Plain, Mont Ventoux, the hills of the Lubéron and the Alpilles, follow the path that climbs Colline St-Jacques from the Roman Arch (re-erected here in 1880) at place François-Tourel. On the hill you will find the 12th-century Chapelle St-Jacques, on the site of a temple to Jupiter. Cavaillon's main historic monument is the Cathédrale St-Véran, though the town also contains a richly decorated synagogue and small museum. The latter reflect the town's long-standing links with the Jewish religion, for Cavaillon was one of four Jewish centres – along with Avignon, Carpentras and L'Isle-sur-la-Sorgue – in the Comtat Venaissin, the land given to the papacy by France in 1274.

Cathédrale St-Véran

This Romanesque cathedral dates from the end of the 12th century. It was built in the same elegant style as Avignon's Cathédrale Notre-Dame-des-Doms. *Along place Voltaire.*

Musée Archéologique

Housed in the old hospital chapel, the museum is devoted to local prehistory and the Gallo-Roman period. Exhibits include preserved Gaulish food. *At the intersection of Grand Rue and cours Gambetta. Open: 10am–noon, 2–6pm. Closed: Tuesday. Admission charge.*

Cavaillon is 24km southeast of Avignon.

CHÂTEAUNEUF-DU-PAPE

Châteauneuf-du-Pape was the summer retreat of the 14th-century Avignon popes. The remains of their château overlook the Rhône Valley. Only one tower and a stretch of walls survive. Most visitors are attracted by the area's

Châteauneuf-du-Pape, a place synonymous with fine wines

The jagged profile of the Dentelles de Montmirail, a challenge to rock climbers

highly refined wines (the popes are thought to have established the first vineyards here). There is a bemusing choice of *domaines* where you can taste this prized wine, which benefits from a favourable microclimate and a ground cover of large rounded pebbles that enables the grapes to reach a very high degree of maturity.

Near by, on the opposite bank of the Rhône, is Roquemaure, another wine village with papal connnections, well-preserved old houses, a 13th-century church and a ruined castle.

Musée du Père Anselme

The museum traces the history of wine in the area, with displays of medieval equipment (includes a free wine tasting). *Caves Laurent Charles Brotte. Tel: 90.83.70.07. Open: 9am–noon, 2–6pm. Closed: January and February. Free.*

Châteauneuf-du-Pape is on the D17 between Avignon and Orange.

DENTELLES DE MONTMIRAIL

This striking line of hills flanks the eastern side of the Rhône Valley for 15km between Vaison-la-Romaine and Beaumes-de-Venise. Rising to 734m, they should theoretically be dwarfed by the nearby 1,909m summit of Mont Ventoux. Yet their strange, fiercely jagged profile – a complete contrast to Ventoux's smooth, uniform mass – imparts a presence almost matching that of their lofty neighbour.

The range takes its name from *dentelle*, meaning lace: the needle-sharp peaks and spikes of limestone rock, forced upright by the movement of the earth's crust and eroded by the wind, were thought to resemble the pins on a lacemaking board. Their white-grey summits, rising above slopes and hidden valleys covered in a thick coat of pine, oak and scrub, attract walkers, climbers, naturalists and painters – and, in autumn, seekers of wild mushrooms.

While it is best to explore the Dentelles on foot, the D90 linking Beaumes-de-Venise with Malaucène is a spectacularly scenic road that loops through the mountains. The western slopes are dotted with famous Côtes-du-Rhône wine villages – Gigondas, Vacqueyras, Sablet and Séguret.

Fontaine de Vaucluse where the River Sorgue emerges from its underground source

FONTAINE DE VAUCLUSE

Few visitors see Fontaine de Vaucluse at its most spectacular. The best time to visit this dramatic natural phenomenon is in the winter or spring, when the source of the River Sorgue, fed by rainwater from the Vaucluse Plateau above, rises from a deep hole at the base of a sheer cliff and tumbles over giant boulders down a narrow ravine.

But even in summer, when the source has retreated to a still, ominous pool beneath the cliff face leaving the riverbed above bone dry, it is still an awesome sight. The Vaucluse Fountain is one of the most powerful resurgent springs in the world (it can pump water over its lip at the rate of 150,000 litres per second) and has been traced underground to a depth of over 300m by a remote-controlled submarine.

Fontaine de Vaucluse's magnetic personality has attracted the inevitable clutch of gift shops and souvenir stalls, which line the riverside walk from the car parks to the resurgence. Summer crowds can be a problem, so plan your visit for early in the day – or lunchtime, if you can stand the heat. On your way to the resurgence call in at the paper mill, where high-quality paper is still made the traditional way with the help of a giant waterwheel.

Le Monde Souterrain de Norbert Casteret (The Underground World of Norbert Casteret)

This riverside visitor centre, in which an underground cave system has been re-created, explains the local speleology and the discoveries made at the fountain. *Tel: 90.20.34.13. Open: daily May to August, 10am–noon, 2–6pm; February to April, September and October, Wednesday to Sunday, 10am–noon, 2–5pm. Admission charge. (Conducted tours in French.)*

Musée Pétrarque

Documents and books relating to the life of the 14th-century poet Petrarch can be seen in this small museum, together with a collection of modern art.

Rive gauche de la Sorgue. Tel: 90.20.37.20. Open: Wednesday to Monday mid-April to mid-October, 10am–noon, 2–6.30pm. Closed: mid-October to mid-April. Admission charge.

Fontaine de Vaucluse is on the D25, 24km southeast of Carpentras.

GORDES

Gordes is almost too good to be true. Overlooking the blue hills of the Lubéron, this village of honey-coloured stone houses clings to a south-facing cliff on the edge of the Vaucluse Plateau. Renovated rustic dwellings, villas and discreet hotels, each one complete with the obligatory swimming pool, help create an idyllic vision of Provençal life.

Gordes's film-set appearance hints appropriately at its status: the village is much favoured by the French élite – actors, politicians, media personalities and artists. This status is confirmed by the breathtaking property prices displayed in the local *immobiliers* (estate agents).

Despite its chic nature, Gordes's historic fabric shines through. From the medieval château in the centre of the village, steep cobbled alleyways, lined with an incongruous mixture of fashionable boutiques, immaculate holiday homes and yet-to-be restored houses, weave a confusing path down the precipitous hillside.

Abbaye de Sénanque

The medieval abbey, one of three founded by the Cistercians in Provence, is still in use and also open to the public.
About 4km north of Gordes on the D177. Tel: 90.72.02.05. Open: 10am–noon,

2–6pm (until 5pm in winter). Closed: Sunday morning. Admission charge.

Château de Gordes

This solid-looking castle, flanked by round corner towers, dates from 1031 and was rebuilt in 1525. The castle's Renaissance interior houses the Musée Didactique Vasarely, which displays the work of Hungarian artist Victor Vasarely (see also the Fondation Vasarely in Aix, page 53).
Village centre. Tel: 90.72.02.89. Open: 10am–noon, 2–6pm. Closed: Tuesday. Admission charge.

Village des Bories

Although the *bories* (dry-stone huts) in this amazing village and museum of rural life are prehistoric in appearance, they were in fact built between 200 and 500 years ago. The curving, cone-like roofs display craftsmanship of the highest order.
About 3km southwest of Gordes off the D2 (signposted). Tel: 90.72.03.48. Open: daily 9am–sunset. Admission charge.

Gordes is off the D2, 20km west of Apt.

The Abbaye de Sénanque is being restored by the Cistercians, who founded it in 1148

Orange

*V*isitors arrive with preconceptions of a Roman town *par excellence* and are never disappointed with Orange's awesome Théâtre Antique (amphitheatre) and wonderfully decorative Arc de Triomphe Roman archway. But take these ancient monuments away, and you are left with a fairly ordinary Provençal town blessed with a traffic system that defies any form of logic.

The medieval heart of Orange, just north of the Théâtre Antique, is a pleasant place with open, fountained squares, cafés and shops, though it lacks the personality of other old town centres in this part of the world. To the south, on a high bluff above the Théâtre Antique, is the Parc de la Colline St-Eutrope, with a beautiful viewpoint overlooking the town, the rich vineyards of the Rhône Plain, and the Marcoule nuclear power station. This outcrop was the site of a castle (now in ruins) of the princes of

Orange-Nassau, destroyed in 1663.

The town's name has nothing to do with fruit-growing but derives from the period when it was passed to William the Silent, Prince of Orange, ruler of the Netherlands, in the 16th century.

Despite the name, it was in another, much earlier era that Orange's true identity was established. The Romans founded a colony here in 35BC, leaving the town with a unique legacy – an amphitheatre said to be the best-preserved Roman theatre in the world. We have Maurice, son of William the Silent, to thank for its survival, for he incorporated the theatre's massive wall into the town's fortifications. Orange's Arc de Triomphe is another remarkable survivor.

Arc de Triomphe
Built in about 20BC, this triple-arched monument stands 22m high and is decorated with scenes recalling the Roman conquest of Gaul.
On the northern approach to the town – follow avenue de l'Arc de Triomphe from the centre.

Cathédrale Notre-Dame-de-Nazareth
This Romanesque cathedral, originally founded in 529, suffered great damage

Captured Gauls are portrayed on the 1st-century BC Roman triumphal arch in Orange

Orange's great Roman theatre is still in use, notably for the town's summer music festival

during the 16th-century Wars of Religion. Look out for the ancient carvings on the south porch.
Along rue Notre-Dame off rue Victor-Hugo.

Musée Municipale

Exhibits from Orange's Roman and medieval past include a fascinating Roman land survey and artefacts from the ruined castle. Local traditions and painting are also represented.
Rue Madeleine-Roch. Tel: 90.51.18.24. Open: April to September, Monday to Saturday 9am–6.30pm, Sunday 9am–noon, 2–6.30pm; October to March, 9am–noon, 1.30–5.30pm. Admission charge.

Théâtre Antique (Roman Amphitheatre)

This theatre, built during the reign of Augustus, is an awesome sight. Looking down from the steep-sided semicircle of terraced seats to the stage, you gaze at virtually the same backdrop that must have caught the imagination of audiences 2,000 years ago. The stage wall still stands 36m high, decorated with columns, niches, frescos and a large, suitably imperious statue of Augustus. The theatre's superb acoustics continue to be put to good use. Audiences of 10,000 gather here during Orange's famous summer festival of opera and choral music, though today's patrons are not seated according to rank.

Beside the amphitheatre are the ruins of a huge gymnasium, baths and temple complex, almost 400m long by 80m wide, with three 180m running tracks and a raised platform for gladiatorial combat.
Place des Frères-Mounet. Tel: 90.34.70.88. Open: daily April to September, 9am–6.30pm; October to March, 9am–noon, 1.30–5pm. Admission charge.

a superb viewpoint overlooking the
Vaucluse Plateau, Mont Ventoux, the
Coulon Valley and the Lubéron
Mountains. From vantage points south
and southeast of the village, you can gaze
over the Aiguilles du Val des Fées
(Needles of Fairies' Valley) and the
Chaussée des Géants (Giant's
Causeway), jagged and strangely
weathered areas of rust-red rocks and
cliffs.

*Roussillon is off the N100, about 10km
northwest of Apt.*

RUSTREL COLORADO

The explosive intensity of colours in the
abandoned, canyon-like ochre quarries of
Rustrel Colorado has to be seen to be
believed. Ranging from blood-red to
bright yellow, exposed cliff faces and
weathered pinnacles consisting entirely
of crumbly, sandy rock fill the valley
south of the village of Rustrel. A number
of trails lead into this other-worldly
place. The easiest access is from the car
parks beside the River Doua southwest
and southeast of Rustrel, starting points
for well-defined paths into the Colorado.

*Rustrel Colorado is off the D22, about 8km
northeast of Apt.*

SAULT

Standing at an exhilarating 765m, Sault
displays yet another of Provence's many
faces. On the high, open Vaucluse
Plateau with sweeping vistas westwards
to Mont Ventoux, Sault and its
surroundings have an almost Alpine air.
The fields beneath this unpretentious,
easy-going village are a patchwork of
purple in high summer, when the
lavender is in full bloom. The entire

ROUSSILLON

Roussillon's architecture is a mirror
image of its surroundings. The deep
reds, yellows, rusty oranges and other
burnished tones of its houses reflect the
different shades of ochre rock found in
its surrounding hills. This area's soft
rocks have been quarried and mined
since prehistoric times for their natural
dye. Mining peaked in the late 1920s,
when 40,000 tons of ochre were exported
from the region. By the early 1950s the
industry was in terminal decline, and the
last ochre was mined in Roussillon in
1958.

The village's vibrantly coloured
dwellings, arranged haphazardly in
narrow, winding streets around a
pronounced hill, have given it a new
lease of life: Roussillon is now a place
that everyone wants to see, paint and
photograph. Park your car at the
approach and follow rue de l'Arcade to

Essential oil of lavender, on sale at a roadside stall, is one of the products of Sault

village is swamped in its sweet fragrance during the annual Lavender Festival, held in mid-August. Lavender cultivation and distillation is an important part of the local economy. So too is the manufacture of nougat. The Boyer family of Sault claim that their nougat, not the better-known Montélimar variety, is the real thing.

Sault is on the eastern approach to Mont Ventoux, 41km east of Carpentras.

SÉGURET

Séguret is one of those impossibly picturesque villages that only the French seem capable of creating. Mellow, wheat-coloured houses with terracotta tiled roofs cling to a steep slope above the vineyards of the northern Vaucluse. So well is Séguret integrated into its surroundings that when the sun strikes directly on to its stonework it almost disappears, chameleon-like, into the rocky background of the Dentelles de Montmirail (see page 33).

The village's ridiculously narrow streets were not made for cars. From the car park at the western approach, walk up into the village through the ancient gateway to the 15th-century Mascarons Fountain. Over the last decade or so, Séguret has been 'discovered' by artists and visitors, yet it has managed to avoid the commercial excesses of other hill villages. A medieval atmosphere still pervades its cobbled alleyways, vaulted passageways, nooks and crannies. Each Christmas the 12th-century church is decorated with *santons*, intricately detailed figurines depicting the Nativity (see page 125). *Santons* and Séguret go together: there are a number of makers in the village, one of whom has an enchanting display of *santons* from around the world.

Séguret is off the D977, 10km southwest of Vaison-la-Romaine.

Golden-stoned square and fountain in the unspoilt medieval village of Séguret

LAVENDER AND FLOWERS

The flowers of Provence are amongst its greatest treasures. Their heady mix of colours and scents makes a vivid impression on the senses, not only catching the eye of the casual observer but providing inspiration for the artist and a fertile field of study for the naturalist.

Nature is at its most prodigal in April and May, when sheets of spring flowers cloak the fields and hills. High summer brings out the gaudy brilliance of the sunflower, which Van Gogh captured so well on canvas. But it is typical of the sheer unexpectedness of Provence that the region should also harbour the delicate beauty of the arctic flora that clings to the upper slopes of Mont Ventoux, despite the Mediterranean influences at the foot of the mountain.

THE SCENT OF LAVENDER

It is, perhaps, the lavender that imprints itself most vividly upon the memory of the visitor. In this sun-soaked region it

During World War II, when the French Resistance wanted a name that would symbolise their indomitable toughness, they turned to the hardy scrub plants of Provence, and called themselves the *Maquis*.

grows abundantly, staining the fields a delicate purple and scenting the air in July and August. This pungent scent is captured second-hand in the perfumes of Provence. Golden mimosa, jonquils, roses, thyme, violets and yellow broom are also gathered – some would say plundered – to provide the raw material for the perfumer's art. The flower markets also do a brisk trade in the towns and villages of Provence, and mimosa is cultivated for export in winter.

HIDDEN AWAY

The *maquis* – not a single plant, but a community of dense Mediterranean brush – half-conceals an amazing variety of floral life, including rosemary and juniper, tree heathers and broom. Orchids are plentiful in some districts. The herbs of Provence have not only played a central role in regional cuisine, but have traditionally provided remedies for many an ill.

No self-respecting resort is without that symbol of the Côte d'Azur, the palm tree. Other subtropical and exotic species, in gardens all along the Riviera, also take root in this sunny, sheltered habitat.

The medieval town of Vaison-la-Romaine climbs above the remains of a Roman city

VAISON–LA–ROMAINE

Try to visit Vaison on a Tuesday morning, when the town holds one of the biggest street markets in Provence. Place de Montfort – Vaison's attractive central square – and almost all of the streets leading to it are filled with vendors of fruit, melons and olives, fishmongers, cheesemakers, antique dealers, painters, craftspeople, florists, musicians, entertainers and sellers of humble household items. This colourful, animated gathering is not a show put on for the tourists: markets are a way of life in Provence, and Vaison holds one of the best.

For the rest of the week, Vaison returns to its primary role as a calm and surprisingly cosmopolitan small Provençal town. It is popular with visitors on at least two counts: the town's location, in seductive, rolling countryside between the Rhône Valley and Mont Ventoux, and its underrated, magnificent Roman remains.

The Romans made a comfortable home for themselves in Vaison. You can still wander round the streets of their excavated town, or watch a summer concert in the 7,000-seat amphitheatre. The Romans' single-arched bridge survived the devastating floods in Vaison in the autumn of 1992, when unrelenting storms, held in place by Mont Ventoux, transformed the River Ouvèze into a tidal wave, swamping the lower town.

Vaison's Haute-Ville (Upper Town) was untouched by the floodwater. The

Everything is sold at Vaison's weekly market, which is typical of Provence

rock above the Ouvèze is crowned by an abandoned castle, a wonderful viewpoint accessible by climbing though the narrow, cobbled streets of Old Vaison, a charming and now fashionable place with fountains and fine Renaissance houses.

Ancienne Cathédrale Notre-Dame-de-Nazareth

Built on the foundations of a large Roman monument, this fine cathedral in Provençal Romanesque style dates from the 12th and 13th century. Its beautiful cloisters, attached to its northern wall, are particularly noteworthy.

Avenue Louis-Blanc. Admission charge to cloisters.

Ruines Romaines

Such is the extent of these sprawling ruins that they are split into two sections – Quartier de Puymin and Quartier de la Villasse – divided by the avenue Général de Gaulle, which leads into the town centre. All in all, they give us a rare insight into ordinary, everyday life in the 1st century AD.

Quartier de Puymin, built around a small hill, contains the Théâtre Antique (amphitheatre), the Portique de Pompée (Pompey's Portico), a beautiful colonnaded area that probably served as a public garden, and the remains of residences both modest and grand. The museum, full of finds excavated in Vaison, is also located here.

Quartier de la Villasse contains an amazing paved main street, complete with drains and the remains of shops, together with baths, more gardens, large houses and colonnades.

Accessible off avenue de Général de Gaulle. Tel: 90.36.02.11. Open: daily June to September, 9am–7pm; March to May,

Vaison-la-Romaine shelters the most complete Roman town to be discovered in France

October and November, 9am–6pm; December to February, 9am–5pm. Admission charge.

VÉNASQUE

Vénasque sits astride a steep rock overlooking the Gorges de la Nesque. Its natural defensive position was augmented in medieval times by towers and walls, giving the pretty village an even more self-contained air. Its famous baptistery, probably dating from the 6th century, is one of France's oldest religious buildings. The 13th-century Église de Notre-Dame beside the baptistery is also of interest.

From Vénasque, you can follow a twisting road that climbs over the Vaucluse Plateau to another fascinating religious site, the Abbaye de Sénanque (see page 35). Another place worth visiting nearby is Pernes-les-Fontaines, a working market town that preserves a wonderful array of old monuments, including medieval walls, a tower, gateways, chapels, Renaissance streets and, of course, fountains – 36 in all!

Vénasque is 11km southeast of Carpentras on the D4.

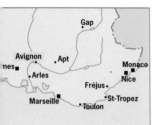

Avignon

Although a large city, Avignon's main places of interest are easily visited on foot, for they are contained within a compact area defined by a ring of walls running continuously for 5km around the city centre. If you are arriving by car, use one of the car parks located alongside the walls.

Pedestrianised shopping streets lead off from the rue de la République, the main thoroughfare through the heart of the walled town. See pages 26–7 for route and more details on the main sites to visit. *Allow at least half a day for the walk, with extra time for a full visit to the Palais des Papes.*

From the Office de Tourisme at 41 cours Jean-Jaurès (tel: 90.82.65.11) walk along rue Joseph Vernet.

1 RUE JOSEPH VERNET

This street is one of the most elegant in Avignon, along which you will pass restaurants and expensive shops selling *haute couture* and high-class confectionery. The Musée Calvet and the Musée Requien are located side by side on the street.

Continue along rue Joseph Vernet towards place Crillon.

2 PLACE CRILLON

Place Crillon's furniture shops sell exclusive antique and modern pieces. Porte de l'Oulle, a gateway in the town walls, leads to the main road bridge over the Rhône.

At the far end of rue Joseph-Vernet, turn right, then first right into rue Petite Fusterie (the antique dealers' quarter), then turn left into rue St-Agricol.

3 ÉGLISE ST-AGRICOL

Église St-Agricol is located along the street of the same name. Dating from the 14th to 16th centuries, it is dedicated to

Relaxing in Avignon's place de l'Horloge

Carved doors, church of St Pierre, Avignon

Avignon's patron saint. It is one of the city's best Gothic edifices, with a beautifully carved 15th-century façade and fine medieval works of art.
Continue on to the Palais du Roure on rue Collège du Roure at the bottom of the place de l'Horloge.

4 PALAIS DU ROURE

The 15th-century Palais du Roure houses a cultural centre for Provençal studies and a museum of popular art and traditions (open to the public on request, tel: 90.80.80.88). Avignon's café society congregates along the place de l'Horloge, a wide, open space flanked by the City Hall and Opera House.
Rue Villar leads to an even more impressive open space, the place du Palais at the foot of the mighty Palais des Papes (Palace of the Popes) and Cathédrale Notre-Dame-des-Doms. At the far end of the square is the Musée du Petit Palais. From here, little alleyways lead to the famous pont St-Bénézet (signposted). From the bridge, walk alongside the ramparts to the flights of steps that zigzag up the cliff face to the beautiful gardens of Rocher des Doms.

5 JARDINS ROCHER DES DOMS

These restful gardens, set on a high outcrop overlooking Avignon and

neighbouring Villeneuve-lès-Avignon, command wonderful views northwards across the majestic Rhône. This is the perfect place for a picnic, with play areas, an ornamental lake and shady pathways.
Take the Escaliers Ste-Anne (the steps down from the gardens) to rue Banasterie.

6 CHAPELLE DES PÉNITENTS NOIRS

At this point, you can take a short detour northwards along rue Banasterie for the Chapelle des Pénitents Noirs, an 18th-century baroque edifice. Southbound, rue Banasterie leads to place St-Pierre and its church (14th to 16th centuries), noted for its flamboyant Gothic-style façade and huge carved walnut doors. Follow rue des Fourbisseurs to place St-Didier, which, like place St-Pierre, has a fine Renaissance church.
Rue Laboureur and rue Frédéric-Mistral lead to rue de la République and the Musée Lapidaire, which contains archaeological finds from the Egyptian, Greek and Gallo-Roman periods (tel: 90.85.75.38).

Appearances can be deceptive in Avignon

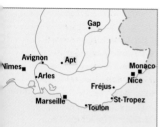

The Lubéron

The Parc Naturel Régional du Lubéron, established in 1977, stretches for over 60km between Cavaillon in the west and Manosque in the east, taking in two *départements* – the Vaucluse and Alpes-de- Haute-Provence (see page 138 for more details). This tour concentrates on the western part of the park – an area dominated by the uplands of the Petit (Small) Lubéron, which rise to 700m – and the picturesque villages that are often perched high on the slopes. *The tour, which at a leisurely pace should take all day, begins at Apt, the region's major town and location of the visitor centre for the park (see page 24).*

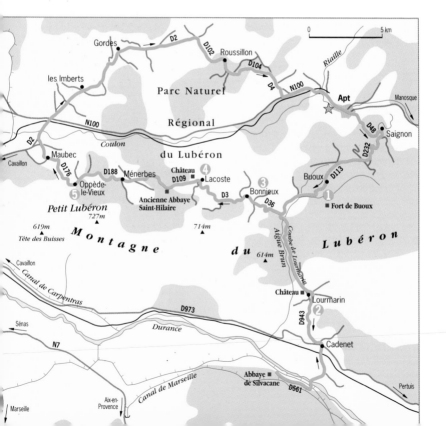

From Apt take the D48 southeast to Saignon, a perched village with a Romanesque church. The D232 and D113 lead south to Buoux and the Fort de Buoux.

1 FORT DE BUOUX

The Fort de Buoux, an abandoned fortified village standing high on a natural platform and accessible by foot, is full of interest. The bastions, ramparts, keep, rock dwellings, 13th-century church and remains of a recently excavated medieval village can all be seen.

Follow the D943 south through the Combe de Lourmarin, the only road to cut through the Lubéron Mountains for 20km on either side, to Lourmarin.

2 LOURMARIN

Writers Henri Bosco (who described the Lubéron Mountains as a 'blue whale') and Albert Camus, who won the Nobel prize for literature in 1957, both lived in this attractive village, which is guarded by a Renaissance château (guided tours available, tel: 90.68.15.23). From here you can take a short detour further south to visit the Abbaye de Silvacane (see page 51).

From Lourmarin, return along the D943, turning left along the D36 to Bonnieux.

3 BONNIEUX

The Provence of Peter Mayle, undoubtedly the Lubéron's best-known writer-in-residence (though there are rumours that his fame has forced him to consider leaving), is populated by simple – and not so simple – country folk. This bucolic picture is not, of course, wholly accurate.

Bonnieux, Lacoste and Ménerbes, which are all featured in his books, are fashionable places that manage to combine sophistication with a certain down-to-earth charm. Bonnieux is a lively, attractive, terraced village situated on a steep hill commanding wonderful views across to Lacoste, Gordes, the Vaucluse Plateau and Mont Ventoux. Its unusual Musée de la Boulangerie (Museum of Baking – tel: 90.75.88.34), converted from an ancient bakery, is worth a visit.

Take the D3/D109 to Lacoste.

4 LACOSTE

Lacoste is famous – or infamous – for its château, home of Donatien Alphonse François, better known as the Marquis de Sade (1740–1814). Take the D109 to Ménerbes, which passes the Ancienne Abbaye St-Hilaire, a 12th-century religious site with a surviving chapel. Ménerbes was the scene of a long siege in the 16th-century Wars of Religion, when it was a Protestant stronghold. Its ancient fortifications are now largely in ruins.

From Ménerbes take the D188 to Oppède-le-Vieux.

5 OPPÈDE-LE-VIEUX

Oppède towers over a wild landscape of rocks and woodland. Another perched village with a past dominated by conflict, it was abandoned at the end of the last century. It has since been rediscovered by artists and intellectuals, who have sympathetically restored its old houses and given the village a new role as an arts and cultural centre.

The D176 leads to the small village of Maubec and onwards to the D2. Cross the N100, staying on the D2 for Gordes (see page 35). From here, continue east on the D2, turning right on the D102 for Roussillon (see page 38). Return to Apt via the D4/N100.

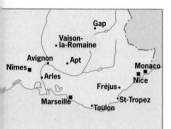

Mont Ventoux

Wherever you travel in the Vaucluse, you take Mont Ventoux with you. This towering landmark, 1,909m high, is visible from all corners, its gleaming white summit of bare rock shimmering against the blue heat haze or suddenly – and ominously – cast into shadow by gathering storm clouds. Mont Ventoux, literally the Windy Mountain, is the intimidating presence in an otherwise seductive Provençal landscape. You would not want to be on Ventoux's summit when the *mistral* is blowing at a brutal 250kph. On the other hand, in sunny, calm weather, the views from the top are truly breathtaking. *Allow at least half a day for the tour.*

From Vaison-la-Romaine (see page 42) take the D938 to Malaucène.

1 MALAUCÈNE
Malaucène's pleasant main street is lined with plane trees, cafés and restaurants. The old town, a maze of alleyways, tall

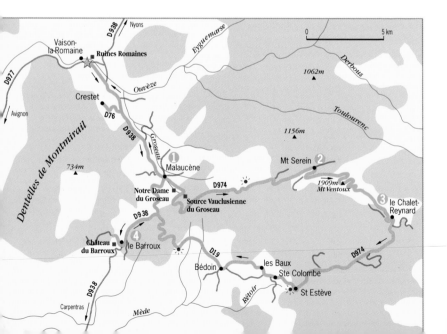

houses and fountains, preserves an authentic Provençal atmosphere. Malaucène's proximity to Mont Ventoux makes it a lively tourist centre in summer and a major base for hiking, riding, and cycling expeditions. A short distance from the town, on the road up to Mont Ventoux, is La Groseau, a spring that emerges from a rocky fissure to form a clear pool surrounded by trees and picnic tables.

The D974 climbs through beautiful wooded countryside on the north-facing slopes of Ventoux. Up until the ski station of Mont Serein, the road is wide, with sweeping, well-engineered bends.

The summit of Mont Ventoux is used for telecommunications, radar and meteorology

2 MONT SEREIN

At 1,445m, Mont Serein is a modest ski resort, busy at weekends in winter with skiers from Avignon (the mountain is usually snow-capped above 1,400m from December to March).

The final climb to the summit of Mont Ventoux from Mont Serein is the most spectacular part of the ascent. The road becomes narrower, the bends more severe – and the drops more vertiginous! For the final 300m or so, the forests of pine, oak, cedar, beech and larch give way to a bare expanse of broken rock, a strange, barren environment. Stranger still are the monumental buildings and sinister-looking installations on the summit; these are used for tele-communications, air force radar and meteorological purposes. The panorama from the top is one of the best in Europe. On a clear day, looking down into the valley of the Toulourenc or across to the jagged peaks of the Alps gives a fleeting impression of flight.

From the summit, the D974 descends to Le Chalet-Reynard, Ventoux's smaller, southern ski station.

3 LE CHALET–REYNARD

Before Le Chalet-Reynard, you will see a small roadside monument, usually garlanded by cycle tyres and inner tubes. This shrine is a homage to British cyclist Tommy Simpson, who suffered heart failure here on 13 July 1967 while competing in the Tour de France. It was one of the hottest days ever recorded in the race.

Continue on the D974 to Bédoin (see page 30) and the scenic D19, which brings you to the D938. Here, you can take a short detour south to Le Barroux.

4 LE BARROUX

The restored Château du Barroux (tel: 90.60.79.94), dating from the 12th century and remodelled in the 16th, stands on a rocky outcrop overlooking the village.

On the way back to Vaison, take another short detour along the D76 for Crestet, a picturesque village perched high above the valley of the Ouvèze. Hidden in the slopes beyond the village is a fascinating collection of woodland sculptures.

Bouches-du-Rhône

*B*ordered by the Durance to the north and the Rhône to the west, the Bouches-du-Rhône is one of the oldest inhabited regions of Provence, with some of the best monuments from Roman and medieval times. The mighty Rhône meets the Mediterranean amongst the reedy flatlands of the Camargue, a truly distinctive part of Provence with an identity all of its own. Elsewhere in this varied *département* there are low hills, fertile landscapes, busy commercial waterfronts and the first intimations of the glamorous Riviera coast.

BOUCHES-DU-RHÔNE

Pont du Gard · Remoulins · Avignon · le Thor · Gordes
Montfavet · l'Isle-sur-la-Sorgue · Fontaine de Vaucluse
Barbentane · Châteaurenard · Noves
D999 · N106 · D999 · Boulbon · Abbaye St-Michel-de-Frigolet · Ménerbes
Nîmes · Beaucaire · Tarascon · St-Rémy-de-Provence · Orgon · Cavaillon · Montagne
N113 · D99 · Chaîne des Alpilles · les Baux-de-Provence · Eygalières · Sénas · Durance
A9/E15 · Fontvieille · Aqueducs · Eyguières · Grottes de Calès · N7
Gallargues-le-Montueux · Vistre · N113 · A54 · Abbaye-de-Montmajour · Arles · Salon-de-Provence · Château de la Barben
Lunel · Château de Teillan · Vauvert · St-Gilles · N572 · N113/E80 · Miramas · A7/E80 · N113
Canal du Rhône à Sète · Mas du Pont de Rousty · BOUCHES-DU-RHÔNE · N568 · Arc
la Grande-Motte · Albaron · Parc Naturel Régional de Camargue · Rhône · Rognac
Aigues-Mortes · Pt Méjanes · Étang de Vaccarès · Istres · Étang de Berre · Berre-l'Étang
le Grau-du-Roi · Château d'Avignon · Camargue · Port de Fos · Fos-sur-Mer · Martigues · Marignane
Parc ornithologique du Pont de Gau · A55
Saintes-Maries-de-la-Mer · Salin-de-Giraud · Port-St-Louis-du-Rhône
Pointe du Sablon · Carro
Cap Couronne · Carry-le-Rouet

Golfe du Lion

0   10   20   30 km

ABBAYE-DE-MONTMAJOUR

You will have no difficulty in spotting this imposing ruin, which occupies a slight rise in the Rhône delta's flatlands northeast of Arles. Looking more military than religious, it was founded in the 10th century by the Benedictines, an industrious group of monks who set about draining and reclaiming the marshlands of this low-lying area. In 1791, after a troubled few centuries, the abbey was sold and its assets stripped. Luckily, the people of Arles adopted the building in the 19th century, restoring it little by little.

Much remains from the abbey's early period: a 12th-century church with a fine vaulted crypt, cloisters (again 12th-century, but rebuilt in later times), monastic buildings, a tall, castellated abbey tower constructed to defend the abbey in 1369 and, next door to the tower, a tiny chapel carved out of the hillside.

On the D17 between Arles and Fontvieille. Tel: 90.54.64.17. Open: April to September, 9–11.45am, 2–7pm; October to March, till 5pm. Admission charge.

ABBAYE DE SILVACANE

This 12th-century abbey is one of the Cistercians' 'three Provençal sisters' – the others being Sénanque (see page 35) and Thoronet (see page 136). From its setting above the River Durance, just a few kilometres from the village of La Roque-d'Anthéron, it looks across to the foothills of the Lubéron.

The abbey's plain, uncluttered lines reflect the Cistercians' firm belief in simplicity. Its church, built into a steep slope, is devoid of any decoration. The daily routine of the monks is brought to life in some of the abbey's other buildings, which include a library, chapterhouse, warming house, dormitory and large refectory complete with pulpit. Following a period of decline, it became the village church for La Roque-d'Anthéron in the early 16th century, but was later abandoned.

On the D561, northeast of Salon-de-Provence). Tel: 42.50.41.69. Open: April to September, daily 9am–7pm; October to March, 9am–noon, 2–5pm (closed Tuesday in winter). Admission charge.

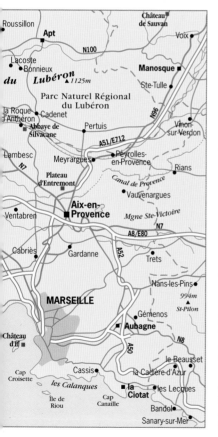

Aix-en-Provence

*T*ake a stroll along cours Mirabeau on a warm summer's day and you could be forgiven for thinking that you are in Paris. The wide street, lined with pavement cafés, plane trees, mossy fountains and handsome 17th- and 18th-century buildings, must surely have been built for promenading. It captures the spirit of a city that is both youthful and dignified, stimulating and calming, stylish and historic. It is cosmopolitan, yet utterly French.

Aix, more than any other city in Provence, has an air of completeness. This may have something to do with its splendid situation poised between country and coast, with none of the rusticity of the former or the crass commercialism of the latter. It may also be due to a well-balanced blend of age groups – the youth of Aix's large student influx balanced against an affluent, worldly resident population. Whatever the reasons, it is a winning formula.

The city authorities have further enhanced Aix's intrinsic appeal by treating the historic centre with loving care and attention.

The fountain centrepiece of la Rotonde at the entrance to old Aix-en-Provence

Wherever you look, you will be reminded of Aix's historic status as capital of Provence, a position it held from the 12th century to the French Revolution. Start your exploration at La Rotonde, a monumental roundabout with a fabulous fountained centrepiece. From here, walk along cours Mirabeau, which more or less acts as the southern boundary to Aix's historic heart (though the Mazarin Quarter, built between 1645 and 1651 by Archbishop Michel Mazarin, lies further south again).

Take any of the streets north and you are soon in the Aix of old. Place d'Albertas, for example, has a lovely cobbled courtyard and fountain flanked by 18th-century houses with wrought-iron balconies. Place Richelme, the site of a daily vegetable market, is another pleasant open space, next door to the even more spacious place de l'Hôtel de Ville. There are, perhaps, too many immaculate open spaces to appreciate them all in one visit. Architecture buffs will be similarly satiated with an overload of richly decorated 16th- to 18th-century mansions – the Hôtel de Ville, for instance, its classical features carved into warm stone.

Atelier Cézanne (Cézanne's Studio)
Impressionist painter Paul Cézanne (1839–1906) was inspired by the light, colour and surroundings of his

Under the shade of the plane trees of cours Mirabeau is the place to see and be seen in Aix

birthplace, Aix. His studio has been left as it was at his death.
9 avenue Paul-Cézanne. Tel: 42.21.06.53. Open: Wednesday to Monday, summer 10am–noon, 2.30–6pm; winter 10am–noon, 2–5pm. Admission charge.

Cathédrale St-Sauveur
Spanning the 5th to 16th centuries, this fascinating religious site – a mixture of ornate and restrained influences – is a lesson in ecclesiastical architecture. Filled with medieval art treasures, it also boasts delightful Romanesque cloisters displaying spiralling, flowing stone-carving of the highest order.
At the north end of rue Gaston-de-Saporta.

Fondation Vasarely
The exciting work of 20th-century artist Victor Vasarely is difficult to categorise. A visit to his arts and architecture centre (and his 'didactic museum' at Gordes – see page 35) is a stimulating experience.
Avenue Marcel-Pagnol, Jas-de-Bouffan. Tel: 42.20.01.09. Open: 9.30am–12.30pm, 2–5.30pm. Closed: Tuesday from September to June. Admission charge.

Musée d'Histoire Naturelle
Its important collections include rare dinosaur eggs.
6 rue Espariat. Tel: 42.26.23.67. Open: 10am–noon, 2–6pm. Closed: Sunday morning. Admission charge.

Musée des Tapisseries (Tapestry Museum)
Famous tapestries and panels are displayed in a former archbishops' palace.
28 place des Martyrs-de-la-Résistance. Tel: 42.21.05.78. Open: Wednesday to Monday 10am–noon, 2–6pm. Admission charge.

Musée du Vieil Aix (Museum of Old Aix)
The museum recalls Aix's aristocratic past and popular traditions.
17 rue Gaston-de-Saporta. Tel: 42.21. 43.55. Open: Tuesday to Sunday 10am–noon, 2.30–5pm (until 6pm in summer). Admission charge.

Arles

*V*isitors attracted to Arles on the strength of the town's Roman past and the canvases of Vincent Van Gogh, its most celebrated resident, might expect to find a surfeit of upmarket shops and expensive cafés. Refreshingly, the town wears its fame lightly. Although the streets are packed full of monuments and museums, Arles maintains an honest, everyday quality. The Romans established a major base here and the town continued to prosper in medieval times, when it was an important trading and religious centre and base for the Counts of Provence. Vincent Van Gogh arrived in Arles in 1888 and was soon singing its praises to his colleague Paul Gauguin.

The Alyscamps
Wooded avenues of ancient tombs and mausoleums line this early Christian necropolis southeast of the town centre.
Avenue des Alyscamps.

Arènes (Roman Amphitheatre)
This enormous oval, dating from the end of the 1st century, became a fortress in medieval times and was later transformed into a small township of 200 houses. Nineteenth-century restoration has largely returned it to its former glory, though its third floor has completely disappeared. There are fine views from its main tower into an arena, which these days is a popular venue for bullfighting.
Rond-Point des Arènes. Tel: 90.18.41.20. Open: June to September, 9am–12.30pm, 2–7pm; March, April, May and October, 9am–12.30pm, 2–6pm; November to February, 9am–noon, 2–5pm. Admission charge.

Cathédrale St-Trophime
The cathedral's main doorway is probably the most accomplished example of 12th-century Provençal stonecarving in existence. The elaborate decorations are, quite literally, of biblical proportions. Amongst the episodes and people depicted are Christ's birth, the

Last Judgement, the Twelve Apostles and the condemned being led to hell.
Place de la République. Cathedral open: 10am–noon, 2–7pm. Cloisters open: June to September, 9am–12.30pm, 2–7pm; April and May, 9.30am–12.30pm, 2–7pm; rest of year, 10am–12.30pm, 2–5.30pm. Admission charge.

Fondation Vincent Van Gogh
Works by leading contemporary artists, sculptors and photographers pay homage here to the great painter.
Palais de Luppé, 26 Rond-Point des Arènes. Tel: 90.49.94.04. Open: daily 10am–12.30pm, 2–7pm. Admission charge.

Musée Lapidaire d'Art Chrétien (Museum of Christian Art)
This museum contains one of the world's best collections of carved sarcophagi, rivalling that of the Vatican. The museum's Cryptoporticus is a huge undergound Roman gallery.
Rue Balze. For telephone and opening details see the Arènes. Admission charge.

Musée Réattu
Founded by the painter Réattu (1760–1833), the museum is famous for its Picassos. Other galleries contain collections of modern and contemporary

art, together with exhibitions of photography.
Rue du Grande Prieuré. Tel: 90.49.37.58.
For opening details see the Cloisters,
Cathédrale St-Trophîme. Admission charge.

Museon Arlaten

Poet Frédéric Mistral established this museum at the turn of the century. Its furnishings, costumes, documents and everyday items reflect traditional Provençal life, crafts and customs.
Rue de la République. Tel: 90.96.08.23.
Open: summer 9am–noon, 2–7pm (5pm in winter). Closed: Monday, October to June. Admission charge.

Théâtre Antique (Roman Theatre)

The name is misleading. There is not much antiquity left at this open-air theatre, but it is nonetheless a pleasant venue for summer performances.
Close to the Arènes. For telephone and opening details see the Arènes. Admission charge.

Thermes de Constantin (Baths of Constantine)

Dating from the 4th century, these baths are all that remain of a Roman palace.
Rue Dominique-Maïsto. For telephone and opening details see the Arènes. Admission charge.

ARLES

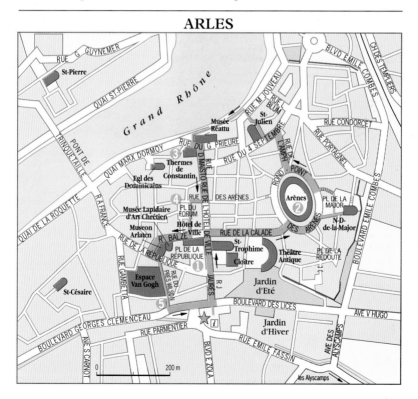

VAN GOGH

The name of the Dutch painter Vincent Van Gogh (1853–90) is ineradicably linked with Provence. The region shimmers with heightened colour and vibrancy in the loud, swirling canvases he painted here towards the end of his troubled life.

Van Gogh, the son of a pastor, trained for the ministry himself, but was reproached for 'excessive zeal' by his superiors when he gave many of his possessions to the poor. He decided to become an artist and was kept alive principally by a regular allowance from his younger brother Théo.

THE LURE OF THE SOUTH

Self-taught as an artist, he was influenced by the new French Impressionist movement led by Monet, Renoir and Degas and lived in the Montmartre area of Paris for two years. He then moved to the South of France, bewitched by its dazzling light and colours, and rented a house in Arles in 1888. Inspired by the idea of an artists' colony, he persuaded his friend Paul Gauguin to join him, but the two soon fell out. After a fierce row, Van Gogh cut off the lobe of his right ear and sent it to a prostitute in an envelope.

BLOSSOMING CREATIVITY

Despite – or perhaps because of – his emotional state, his 14 months in Arles were the most productive of his life. During this short period, he produced hundreds of paintings and drawings. Van Gogh was never popular in the town, where he was jeered at as a 'madman', and none of his works can be found in the local art museums. The sunflowers and cypresses he depicted so vividly still grow in abundance, however, and his personal experience of Provence is captured in such works as the portrait of his friend Roulin the postman, his painting of his bedroom in Arles, and the swirling colours of his magical *Starry Night* series.

In 1889, fear of madness prompted him to commit himself voluntarily to an asylum in St-Rémy-de-Provence, where he was allowed to paint in the gardens. Later he moved to Auvers-sur-Oise in northern France, but shot himself in the chest in July 1890.

Left: the famous
Sunflowers
Right: memorial to the
artist in Arles

VINCENT
VAN-GOGH
1853 · 1890

Les Baux-de-Provence

*A*t the last count, 1½ million visitors poured through the entrance to Les Baux each year, making it one of Provence's most popular attractions, so it does get extremely busy. Nonetheless, to miss Les Baux is to miss a unique and stirring site. In a country of countless fortified towns and villages, it ranks among the finest. Its size alone makes it special. Les Baux occupies a narrow spur of land almost 1km long, flanked by sheer-sided cliffs. But this offshoot of the Alpilles range of hills is not famous simply for its natural attributes.

This protected mini-plateau is the site of a remarkable medieval ghost town. At one time, this citadel was a town of 6,000 inhabitants. Throughout the medieval period, Les Baux and its bellicose independent rulers had a troublesome reputation. In 1632, the French monarchy's patience finally broke and Les Baux's castle and ramparts were demolished, its crestfallen population migrating to land reclaimed from the marshes. It then lay forgotten for centuries until the discovery of bauxite – the aluminium ore that takes its name from the town – in the locality in the 19th century.

Nowadays, Les Baux relies on tourism. The lower village, the 'living town', is the focus of all the commercial attention, though it still contains some fine old buildings. Place St-Vincent is a lovely, shady square, with views across to the Val d'Enfer (Valley of Hell, so called because of its weirdly eroded, jagged countenance). Ranged around the square are the 12th-century Église St-Vincent, the 17th-century Chapelle des Pénitents-Blancs (White Penitents' Chapel: see box), and the 16th-century Hôtel des Porcelets, which displays works of contemporary art. Other notable buildings here include the Hôtel de Manville, a 16th-century building with beautiful Renaissance windows; it now serves as the town hall.

THE PENITENTS

The Middle Ages saw the formation of penitent brotherhoods, mostly charitable organisations patronised by noblemen and even royalty – partly, perhaps, to make a favourable impression through public penance and good deeds and thus to massage their consciences, partly to help each other. Each fraternity had a different-coloured habit and hood, by which they were identified during processions. The White, Grey and Black Penitents all had chapels in Avignon. In the 16th century both Charles IX and Henri III walked barefoot through Avignon in the White hood.

Cathédrale d'Images

A short distance northwest of the village on the D27 is the Cathédrale d'Images. Here, the vast caverns of the old bauxite quarries serve as a unique three-dimensional screen for an inventive sound and light show in which images are projected on to every available surface.

Tel: 90.54.38.65. Open: daily March to November 10am–7pm (until 6pm from late September). Closed: Tuesday.

The atmospheric Ville Morte of Les Baux repays the stiff climb from the town below

Ville Morte

The undoubted highlight of a visit to Les Baux is the Deserted Village, or Ville Morte. This strange place, on the higher ground to the east and south, is a sprawl of stumpy, intriguing remains that seem to grow out of the bare, dazzlingly white limestone rock. The entire area is sealed off, accessible only through the Musée Lapidaire in the lower village (entry by payment). The museum displays artefacts excavated locally together with a presentation of the history of the citadel. On entering the Ville Morte, one of the first sites you come to is the Romanesque Chapelle St-Blaise. From here, walk to the southern tip of the plateau to the

monument of the poet Charloun Rieu. Here you can take in an all-encompassing viewpoint south to Arles and the Camargue as far as Stes-Maries-de-la-Mer.

The main defensive sites are at the opposite end of the plateau, beyond the Tour Sarrasine (Saracen Tower). The shell of Les Baux's once mighty castle, demolished in the 17th century, still captures the imagination (there are more magnificent panoramas from its 13th-century keep and the Tour Paravelle). *Tel: 90.54.55.56. Open: daily March to October, 8am–7pm (8pm in summer); November to February, 9am–6pm (5.30pm in winter). Admission charge.*

Camargue

*T*he Camargue is unique. This strange, flat, lagoon-like delta is an unfathomable mixture of land and water; it is difficult to know where land begins and water ends. The Camargue's major feature is the Étang de Vaccarès, a large lagoon that is the focal point for the Parc Naturel Régional de Camargue. The entire area is bounded by two rivers, the Grand and the Petit Rhône, and riddled with irrigation channels, ditches and dikes.

Aigues-Mortes, built as a port, is still largely contained within its 13th-century ramparts

Human settlement is thin on the ground, confined mainly to the Camargue's hardy *gardians* (herdsmen). Humans apart, this indeterminate environment teems with wildlife. The Camargue is one giant nature reserve, home to stick-legged flamingos and badgers, seabirds and marshbirds, frogs and pond turtles, water snakes and wild boars. To this list is added the famous white horses and the bulls, essential elements in the local Camarguais culture (see page 75). It would be irresponsible not to mention another, less appealing member of the local fauna: the mosquito. In summer, anywhere away from a sea breeze, you will need the protection of a potent insect repellent. The Camargue's mosquitoes have been known to drive strong men crazy!

AIGUES-MORTES

Fortified Aigues-Mortes has a remarkably well-preserved ring of walls. Their survival was due more to benign neglect than anything else, for the town was a forgotten backwater for centuries.

Tour de Constance (Constance Tower) and Ramparts

This 13th-century tower is a massive, 40m-high keep in the northwestern corner of Aigues-Mortes's rectangular fortifications. From the top there is a terrific view across the town and the Camargue.
Tel: 66.53.61.55. Open: October to March, 10am–noon, 2–5pm; April to September, 9am–noon, 2–6pm. Admission charge.

CENTRE D'INFORMATION DU PARC

Based alongside the Étang de Ginès (Ginès Lagoon), this excellent centre illustrates the Camargue's flora and fauna through exhibitions and real life: electric-pink flamingos and other wildlife can be seen from the huge observation window. There are similar centres – La Capelière (tel: 90.97.00.97) and Domaine de la Palissade (tel: 42.86.81.28) – on the eastern side of Étang de Vaccarès.
Pont de Gau. Tel: 90.97.86.32. Open: daily 9am– noon, 2–6pm. Closed: Friday October to March. Free.

Crane and flamingos, very much at home in the watery landscape of the Camargue

and human activity of the area, and has a 3.5km countryside trail.

On the D570 approximately 9km southwest of Arles. Tel: 90.97.10.82. Open: April to September, daily 9.15am–6.45pm (until 6.45pm July and August); October to March, 10am–4.15pm (closed Tuesday). Admission charge.

PARC ORNITHOLOGIQUE DU PONT DE GAU

Alongside the Centre d'Information du Parc, this park has aviaries plus many well-signposted trails for bird spotters.
Tel: 90.97.82.62. Open: daily 8am–sunset. Closed: December and January. Admission charge.

STES-MARIES-DE-LA-MER

This popular seaside resort is too commercialised for some tastes. Its white-painted, boxy dwellings are more reminiscent of Spain than France, an impression reinforced by the flamenco guitarist street musicians. The town is a famous gathering place for the gypsies on 24 and 25 May each year, when they celebrate their patron saint Sarah (see page 154).

CHÂTEAU D'AVIGNON

Take a guided tour of this opulently furnished château, which stands in beautiful grounds.
At Albaron. Tel: 90.97.86.32 for information. Open: daily 10am–4.30pm. Closed: winter. Admission charge.

LA GRANDE-MOTTE

Purpose-built La Grande-Motte is an ultra-modern seaside resort of boldly designed triangular apartment blocks which, on first impression, look as if they would be more at home on a snowy French Alp. On closer acquaintance, the resort is not as intimidating as it appears to be, thanks to imaginative landscaping.

MAS DU PONT DE ROUSTY

The Musée Camarguais is located at this old *mas* (farmhouse). It covers the history

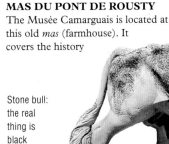

Stone bull: the real thing is black

Summer visitors galore like to relax in the cafés and restaurants of fashionable Cassis

CASSIS

This is where the Côte d'Azur unofficially begins. Cassis, 22km east of Marseille, is at the start of the most exotic, expensive stretch of coastline in Europe. The little resort, by Riviera standards, is understated and unpretentious, though its flower-bedecked streets are as impossibly busy during high summer as everywhere else along the coast.

Visitors come to Cassis for its three beaches, picturesque harbour and idyllic location along a deep, mountain-backed bay. To appreciate this setting to the full, take the spectacular D141 coast road (the route des Crêtes) to La Ciotat and stop off at heart-stopping Cap Canaille – at around 400m, reputedly the highest cliff in continental Europe – which looks down directly into the clear blue-green waters of the bay. Exploration of the inaccessible coastline between Marseille and Cassis is not so easy. This strange, fjord-like shore, known as Les Calanques (see box), can be viewed by boat from Cassis's harbour.

LA CIOTAT

Whereas neighbouring Cassis is tucked snugly into its bay, La Ciotat sprawls lazily along a much more open coastline. La Ciotat is a resort of two halves: the old port, sheltering in the lee of Cap de l'Aigle, and a long sandy beach. The old port might not fulfil everyone's expectations. It still displays all the hallmarks of an unglamorous ship-building past, though some may find such an intrusion of down-to-earth reality refreshing on a coastline that assiduously courts a gilded image.

Beyond the café-lined harbour there lies an old town of considerable interest. Notre-Dame-de-l'Assomption is a grand 17th-century church overlooking the port, and there are chapels dedicated to the Blue and Black Penitents (see page 58). History of a more contemporary kind was made in the beach district in 1895, with the first showing of motion pictures by the Lumière brothers.

Musée Ciotaden

This local museum traces the history of the town from ancient times, when it was an outpost of Marseille.
Ancien Hôtel de Ville, quai Ganteaume. Tel: 42.71.40.99. Open: summer, Monday, Wednesday and Saturday 4–8pm, Sunday 10am–noon; winter 3–6pm, Sunday 10am–noon. Closed: Tuesday and Thursday. Admission charge.

La Ciotat is on the D559 between Marseille and Toulon.

FONTVIEILLE

Forever associated with this small town at the western approach to the Alpilles is the writer Alphonse Daudet (1840–97). His mainly cheerful, ironic stories make him one of the most important humorists

Fine buildings line the old port of La Ciotat, a town that once thrived on shipbuilding

of his time, but his writing also reflected themes critical of society. Although Daudet's *Lettres de Mon Moulin* (*Letters from my Windmill*) were mostly composed in Paris, they were inspired by this locality. The windmill just south of the town contains a small museum dedicated to him. It stands on a summit that commands an excellent panorama northwards to the vast plain of the Rhône and eastwards to the angular Alpilles. At the foot of the hill there are more Daudet associations – in a museum in the Château de Montauban, where Daudet often stayed. (A joint ticket is available for admission to the mill and château – details from the Office de Tourisme, tel: 90.54.70.01.)

Of equal if not more interest in this area are the relatively unknown Roman remains a few kilometres south of Fontvieille. The Aqueducs de Barbegal are an impressive sight. A long line of ruined archways marks the route of the aqueduct, built to supply Arles with water from Eygalières, 50km away. The remains of a large 4th-century flour mill can also be seen.

Fontvieille is on the D17 about 10km northeast of Arles.

LES CALANQUES

This is the name given to the deeply indented limestone shoreline between Marseille and Cassis, a protected area and haven for wildlife. Arid, rugged and remote, Les Calanques are best explored by boat from Cassis. Calanque de Port-Miou and Calanque de Port-Pin (also accessible by footpath from a signposted car park west of Cassis) are the closest of this series of jutting, jagged inlets. The most memorable is the remoter Calanque d'En-Vau, where towering white cliffs plunge precipitously into the sea.

Marseille

*M*arseille, more famous for its association with crime, racism and the *French Connection* films than its ancient roots, is often bypassed by visitors. Yet it is one of France's largest cities and the capital of Provence. As such, it has a vitality, as well as an ancestry, that demands attention.

Very little remains of the Greek harbour colony of *Massalia*, founded in the 6th century BC. From Roman maritime base to the docklands and refineries of the 19th and 20th centuries, it has always been the port that has determined Marseille's cosmopolitan personality. But if the image is one of a murky, menacing waterfront city, then the reality – at least around the Vieux Port (Old Port) – comes as a pleasant surprise.

The Vieux Port is as sunny and animated as any southern city. Leading from the quayside is La Canebière, the city's most famous street, lined with cafés and shops.

Basilique de Notre-Dame-de-la-Garde

The steep climb to this 19th-century church, built in a florid Romano-Byzantine style, is worth it for the wonderful panoramas alone.
On an outcrop high above the port; head uphill and pick up the boulevard André Aune off rue/boulevard Fort Notre-Dame running from quay.

Basilique St-Victor

Marseille's oldest church has a crypt containing a 5th-century basilica.
Place St-Victor.

Cathédrale de la Major

The giant 19th-century neo-Byzantine cathedral, 140m long by 70m high, completely dwarfs its ancient harbinger,

the Romanesque Major Ancienne.
Along avenue Robert Schuman.

Château d'If

This craggy island-fortress, like San Francisco's Alcatraz, was used as a prison for centuries (Edmond Dantés, hero of Alexander Dumas's *The Count of Monte Cristo*, was incarcerated here).
Visits by boat from quai des Belges (tel: 91.55.50.09). Admission charge.

Musée des Beaux-Arts (Museum of Fine Arts)

Art from the 16th to 19th centuries is displayed here. The palace also contains the Musée d'Histoire Naturelle.
Palais Longchamp. Tel: 91.62.21.17. Open: 10am–5pm. Closed: Tuesday, and Wednesday morning. Musée d'Histoire Naturelle – tel: 91.62.30.78; open: 10am–noon, 2–6pm. Closed: Tuesday, and Wednesday morning.

Musée Cantini

This gallery concentrates on 20th-century paintings and sculptures.
19 rue Grignan. Tel: 91.54.77.75. Open: 10am–5pm; Saturday and Sunday noon–7pm. Admission charge.

Musée des Docks Romains

The museum contains remains of a rare Roman warehouse plus other artefacts.
Place Vivaux. Tel: 91.91.24.62. Open: 10am–5pm. Closed: Tueaday. Admission charge.

MARSEILLE

Musée d'Histoire de Marseille
Prehistory to the Gallo-Roman period is covered by this museum. Its most famous exhibit is a Roman merchant vessel, preserved by freeze-drying.
Centre Bourse. Tel: 91.90.42.22. Open: noon–7pm. Closed: Sunday. Admission charge.

Musée de la Marine et de l'Économie
Housed in the magnficent Palais de la Bourse are paintings, models of ships and other objects telling the story of the city's economic history.
Palais de la Bourse. Tel: 91.39.33.33. Open: 10am–noon, 2–6pm. Closed: Tuesday. Free.

Musée du Vieux Marseille
This museum of social history is based at the 16th-century Maison Diamantée.
Rue de la Prison. Tel: 91.55.10.19. Open: 10am–5pm. Closed: Tuesday. Admission charge.

La Vieille Charité
The healthy French appetite for iconoclastic art and architecture is satisfied by a giant golden finger sticking out of the ground at the entrance. A restored 17th-century hospice, designed by Pierre Puget, Vieille Charité's new role is as a centre for the arts and science. Exhibitions and special events are held here, and it is home to the excellent Musée d'Archéologie Méditerranéenne.
Rue de la Charité. Tel: 91.56.28.38. Open: weekdays 10am–5pm, weekends noon–7pm. Admission charge.

Nîmes

Denim originated in the textile mills of Nîmes (*de Nîmes*: denim). Despite the ubiquity of the cloth, the city is more famous as a place of great antiquity, exemplified by its outstandingly well-preserved Arènes (Roman amphitheatre). In recent years Nîmes has attracted much attention for its bold – and sometimes controversial – experiments in urban regeneration with futuristic buildings such as the Carrée d'Art. While there is still some way to go (parts of the city are still in need of care and attention), Nîmes has become a fascinating place for lovers of architecture and art old and new.

Arènes (Roman Amphitheatre)

This vast amphitheatre, dating from the 1st century and one of the best preserved in the whole of the Roman world, is still in regular use for everything from pop concerts to bullfights. Its two-storey façade encloses a complex building of galleries, vaulted passageways and tiered terraces that can accommodate over 20,000 people. Other Roman sites in Nîmes include the Porte Auguste (Augustus's Gate) and Castellum (a water tower), a short distance northeast and northwest of the centre respectively.
Boulevard des Arènes. Tel: 66.76.72.77. Open: daily, summer 9am–7pm; winter 9am–noon, 2–5.30pm. Admission charge.

Cathédrale Notre-Dame et St-Castor

Although dating from 1096, it has been almost totally remodelled and rebuilt over the centuries. Note the preserved frieze in the west front, which depicts scenes from the Old Testament.
Place aux Herbes.

Jardin de la Fontaine

This delightful garden is, for many, the highlight of their visit to Nîmes. Created in 1750 around the spring that gave Nîmes its existence, it is France's first public garden, set against a back-drop of rocky, wooded slopes. On the slopes above stands the Tour Magne, a 34m-high Roman tower commanding spectacular views.
Northwest of city centre. Free admission to the gardens. Tour Magne – open: daily, summer 9am–7pm; winter 9am–5.30pm. Admission charge.

Maison Carrée

This colonnaded Roman temple ('The Square House') is unique for its state of preservation, which belies its age of nearly 2,000 years. Neat and, in spite of its name, rectangular, its purity of line and harmonious proportions have given it a reputation as one of the finest

Nîmes' Roman amphitheatre

temples in the Greek tradition outside Italy. Its interior is currently used to display works of art.

Place de la Maison Carrée. Tel: 66.36.26.76. Open: daily summer 9am–7pm; winter 9am–5.30pm. Free.

Musée Archéologique

If you want to feast your eyes on Roman artefacts, then this is the place to visit. The Musée d'Histoire Naturelle et de Préhistoire (Museum of Natural History and Prehistory – tel: 66.67.39.14) is housed at the same address.

13 bis boulevard Amiral-Courbet. Tel: 66.67.25.57. Open: 11am–6pm. Closed: Monday. Admission charge.

Musée des Beaux Arts

The gallery has a large Roman mosaic, paintings of the French, Italian, Flemish and Dutch schools from the 15th to mid-19th centuries, and modern art exhibitions.

Rue de la Cité Foulc. Tel: 66.67.38.21. Open: 11am–6pm. Closed: Monday. Admission charge.

Musée du Vieux Nîmes (Museum of Old Nîmes)

The museum contains Provençal and Languedocian furniture, pottery, painting and everyday objects.

Place aux Herbes. Tel: 66.36.00.64. Open: 11am–6pm. Closed: Monday. Admission charge.

NÎMES

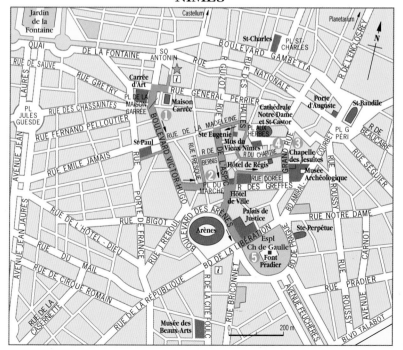

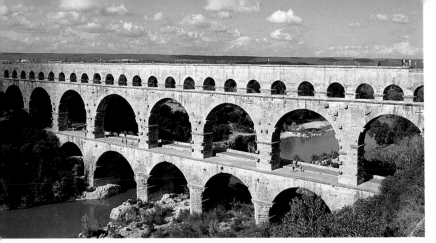
Roman engineering at its most awe-inspiring: the Pont du Gard aqueduct

PONT DU GARD

This 275m-long Roman bridge was constructed in the 1st century to span the Gardon Valley. It was the crowning glory of a 50km aqueduct system of tunnels, ditches, water-regulating basins and other bridges, built to carry water from Uzès to Nîmes. The construction of the Pont du Gard represented a truly monumental feat of engineering. Giant blocks of dressed stone were hoisted and then slotted into place without mortar. Built in three tiers, it has 35 arches along the top directly below the water channel – still visible where covering stones are missing – 11 arches in the middle, and six at the bottom (surprisingly, only one of these bottom arches actually spans the river). The structure towers nearly 50m above the waters of the Gardon, yet possesses a sense of harmony that modern bridge builders seem incapable of replicating. A road built in the 17th century along the east side of the bottom tier carries traffic, forming part of the minor road D981. But the Pont du Gard's really miraculous feature is its state of preservation. Its weathered golden stonework looks good for another 2,000 years, and you get the impression that the bridge could be returned to full working order in a few days.

Visitors constitute the main threat to the Pont du Gard's survival. Currently, access to the site is free and unrestricted. Now, however, a far-reaching preservation plan will safeguard the future of this ancient masterpiece. By about 1996, two new visitor centres will open and, to spread visitor traffic and explain more fully the original aqueduct system, waymarked footpaths will lead to adjoining parts of the excavated watercourse and the quarries that supplied stone for the aqueduct itself. This ambitious programme is fully explained in a temporary exhibition (free admission) near the foot of the bridge.

SALON-DE-PROVENCE

Salon's medieval centre, huddling beneath a rocky hill crowned by the Château de l'Empéri, has seen quite a few changes of late. French architects and town planners have been mostly successful in rejuvenating the heart of the town. New apartments rub shoulders with renovated 16th-century houses, smart shops are beginning to appear in the maze of old streets, and the 13th-century Église St-Michel is having a face-lift. Mercifully, Salon has not been emasculated by this modern development, save at the foot of the château in the place des Centuries, a hopeless open space devoid of life.

Forgetting this one sad mistake, Salon has much to delight the eye. The 18th-century mossy fountain outside the Porte de l'Horloge gateway resembles a giant green toadstool. Along the rue de l'Horloge there is a huge, attention-grabbing mural featuring Michel de Nostradamus (1503–66), the physician/astrologer who spent the last 19 years of his life here. A statue to another famous resident – civil engineer Adam de Craponne (1527–76), whose canal brought water to this previously arid region – stands outside the splendid 17th-century Hôtel de Ville (Town Hall).

Château/Musée de l'Empéri
A military museum of the French armies from Louis XIV to 1914 is housed in the massive castle.
Tel: 90.56.22.36. Open: 10am–noon, 2.30–6.30pm. Closed: Tuesday. Admission charge.

Musée Grevin de la Provence
The history and legends of Provence are imaginatively presented here.
Place des Centuries. Tel: 90.56.36.30. Open: daily, mid-June to mid-September, 10am–noon, 3–8pm; mid-September to mid-June, 10am–noon, 2–6pm. Admission charge.

Musée de Nostradamus
A museum devoted to his work is in the house where this fascinating man lived.
11 rue Nostradamus. Tel: 90.56.64.31. Open: same as Musée Grevin. Admission charge.

Musée de Salon et de la Crau
This local and natural history museum includes a section on the town's soap industry.
Avenue Donnadieu. Tel: 90.56.28.37. Open: Monday to Friday, 10am–noon, 2–6pm; Saturday and Sunday, 2–6pm. Closed: Tuesday. Admission charge.

The fountain near the Porte de l'Horloge in Salon-de-Provence sports a mossy coat

Les Antiques near St-Rémy-de-Provence: detail on the Roman triumphal arch

decorated with beautiful Greek-influenced carvings celebrating the Roman conquest of Marseille. Next to it is one of the world's best-preserved Roman structures, still standing at its full 18m. Although it has always been known as a mausoleum, it is now thought to have been a monument to Lucius and Caius, grandsons of Augustus Caesar. *2km south of the town centre along avenue Vincent-Van-Gogh. Free.*

ST-RÉMY-DE-PROVENCE

St-Rémy is another famous Roman town. Les Antiques – a generic name covering St-Rémy's outstanding commemorative arch and mausoleum – stand side by side a short distance south of the town on the D5 to Les Baux. The arch signalled the entrance to Glanum, an excavated, mainly Roman settlement, one of the most significant ancient sites in France.

The historic centre of St-Rémy itself is compact, charming and self-contained. Nostradamus, whose predictions have intrigued people for centuries, was born along rue Hoche in 1503. Vincent Van Gogh's time in St-Rémy is remembered in the Centre d'Art in the Hôtel Estrine. During his 12-month stay at the St-Paul-de-Mausole psychiatric clinic near Les Antiques, he painted around 150 canvases, including some of his most famous paintings, including *The Starry Night* and *Wheat Field with Cypress*. The building, originally a 12th-century monastery, is still a clinic, with the church and cloisters open to the public (no charge) mornings and afternoons.

Les Antiques

Both monuments are located on the roadside. The triumphal arch is

Centre d'Art

Changing exhibitions of modern works plus a permanent display of Van Goghs can be seen in the beautiful 18th-century Hôtel Estrine. *8 rue Estrine. Tel: 90.92.34.72. Open: 10am–noon, 2–6pm (3–7pm in summer). Closed: Monday. Admission charge.*

Glanum

When Glanum was excavated from 1921 onwards, it revealed evidence of neolithic settlement. Later, in the 2nd century BC, a Gallo-Greek town was established here. But what we see today is mainly Roman, more or less spanning the 1st to 3rd centuries AD. Glanum was an army base, spa town and important crossroads for two major routes between Italy and Spain. The extensive ruins provide a wonderful insight into the life of a thriving Roman city. There are houses, monuments, temples, columns, a forum, canal, fortified gateway, swimming pool, thermal baths and spring. *2km south of the town centre along avenue Vincent-Van-Gogh. Tel: 90.92.23.79. Open: daily, April to September, 9am–7pm; October to March, 9am–noon, 2–5pm. Admission charge.*

Musée des Alpilles

Well-presented displays focus mainly on folk culture, crafts and local traditions.
Place Favier. Tel: 90.92.08.10. Open: daily, July and August, 10am–noon, 3–7pm; April to June, September and October, 10am–noon, 2–6pm; November and December, 10am–noon, 2–5pm. Closed: January to March. Admission charge.

Musée Archéologique

Glanum's excavated artefacts are exhibited here.
Place Favier. Tel: 90.92.13.07. Open: daily April to December, with a complicated range of times that vary daily. Admission charge.

TARASCON

This town on the banks of the Rhône boasts a splendid fairy-tale castle, the Château du Roi René. There must be a special preservative in the air in these parts, for, like St-Rémy near by, Tarascon also merits a 'best-preserved' badge – in this case, for the best-preserved 15th-century castle in France. It rises above the waters of the Rhône to face yet another stirring castle at Beaucaire on the opposite bank.

Château du Roi René

Impregnable defences protect a surprisingly decorative and luxurious interior.
Boulevard du Roy René. Tel: 90.91.01.93. Open: daily, April to September, 9am–7pm; October to March, 9am–noon, 2–5pm. Admission charge.

Tarascon is about 16km west of St-Rémy.

King René's majestic castle beside the River Rhône at Tarascon

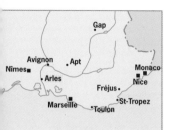

Arles

Arles looks after its walkers well. The places of interest, mostly within a relatively small area, are bounded by the mighty Rhône to the north, the Arènes (Roman amphitheatre) to the east, and the Espace Van Gogh to the west. To make it even easier, all main sites are well signposted. See pages 54–5 for route and more details on the main places to visit. *Allow half a day for the walk, with extra time for museum visits.*

Begin the walk at the Office de Tourisme on boulevard des Lices. Walk along rue Jean-Jaurés to place de la République.

1 PLACE DE LA RÉPUBLIQUE

Place de la République, Arles's central square, is a large, open space where historic architecture, for once, is without the usual

forest of street café parasols. The uncluttered square's impressive dimensions, and the stature of the buildings that surround it, are immediately apparent. Overlooking the fountain and Roman obelisk are the Clock Tower and Hôtel de Ville (Town Hall), its classical 17th-century façade reminiscent of Versailles. To one side is the Ancienne Église Ste-Anne. But the square's chief glory is the wonderfully decorative main doorway of the Cathédrale St-Trophîme.
Rue de la Calade leads to the Théâtre Antique (Roman theatre), Arènes (Roman amphitheatre) and Fondation Vincent Van Gogh.

Espace Van Gogh once sheltered the disturbed artist

2 THE ARÈNES

The Arènes may not seem quite as high as you anticipated: its third storey has disappeared and, adding to its denuded appearance, the pavement around the monument is elevated for much of the way. Halfway around the Arènes, at the place de la Major, visit the Collégiale Notre-Dame-de-la-Major, a Romanesque collegiate church built close to surviving sections of the city ramparts.

Opposite the main steps to the Arènes, follow rue du l'Amphithéâtre, turning left into rue du 4 Septembre. Turn right by the Église St-Julien along rue St-Julien to the riverbank of the Rhône (note the remains of the Roman bridge to the north). A ramped pathway runs along the riverside to the Musée Réattu – the entrance is along rue du Grande Prieuré.

3 THERMES DE CONSTANTIN

Only a short distance from the Musée Réattu are the Thermes de Constantin (Baths of Constantine), accessible along rue Dominique-Maïsto.

Continue along this street for rue de l'Hôtel-de-Ville, turning right into rue des Arènes, which brings you to place du Forum.

Fountain in place de la République: detail

4 PLACE DU FORUM

This small, charming square, lined with cafés and restaurants, is Arles's social hub. On a clear summer's night, it is easy to see where Van Gogh's inspiration for *Café Evening* came from. A statue of Provençal poet and Nobel Prize-winner Frédéric Mistral stands amongst plane trees, close to the Hôtel Nord-Pinus, whose façade partly consists of two columns from a 2nd-century Roman temple.

Leave place du Forum by rue du Palais, turning right along rue Balze for the Musée Lapidaire d'Art Chrétien (Museum of Christian Art). Then turn left into rue Frédéric-Mistral, then left again into rue de la République – one of Arles's main shopping streets – for the Museon Arlaten. Close to the museum, along rue du Président-Wilson, is the Espace Van Gogh.

5 ESPACE VAN GOGH

Espace Van Gogh, inaugurated in 1989, is the old Hôtel-Dieu hospital in which the artist spent time after cutting off his earlobe. It has now been converted into a garden and courtyard with small workshops, all painted in suitably vibrant colours.

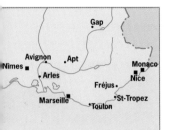

The Camargue

Unlike other parts of Provence, the scenery in the Camargue is not stunning. It is a flat, reedy, marshy and watery place. Here, the wildlife takes priority. You will not even have to look particularly hard, for the prolific birdlife, celebrated white horses and bulls, insouciant in their protected habitat, are all visible from the road. Make sure you leave yourself enough time to experience this area as it should be experienced – on foot or horseback. There are plenty of opportunities for both along the route. See pages 60–1 for more details on the places mentioned here. One final word of advice: theft from cars is particularly rife in this area, so always lock valuables out of sight. *Allow a full day.*

Leave Arles on the D570, stopping off at the Mas du Pont de Rousty, a visitor centre that gives a good, all-round introduction to the Camargue. Continue along the D570 to Albaron, turning left along the D37. After 4km, bear right on the C5 for Méjanes.

1 MÉJANES

Méjanes is a popular spot with visitors. This large complex

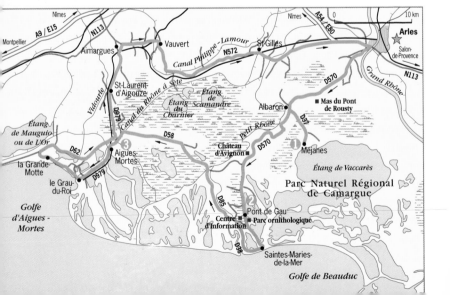

HORSES AND BULLS
The Camargue's white horses come from a distinct breed of unknown origin. Together with the black bulls of the region, they are the mainstay of the local Camarguais culture. The horses, bulls and sheep are looked after by *gardians* (local herdsmen). These hardy, proud Camargue-style cowboys play an important role in maintaining the traditions of the area, often working from a simple windowless thatched dwelling known as a *cabane*. The *gardians* are prominent figures in the summer festivals involving bulls and horses. Many towns and villages hold Provençal-style bullfights, in which the bull survives (always check beforehand to confirm details).

offers horse riding), bullfighting (see box) and rides on a narrow-gauge railway. *Return to the D570, turning left towards Stes-Maries-de-la-Mer. Shortly, you will come to the entrance to the Château d'Avignon. Continue on to Pont de Gau, stopping off at the Centre d'Information du Parc Naturel Régional de Camargue and the next-door Parc Ornithologique.*

2 PONT DE GAU
At Pont de Gau and along the road into Stes-Maries-de-la-Mer, there are many stables at which you can hire horses. Stes-Maries's best beaches, which stretch for many kilometres, are found to the east of the town, and there is a good choice of boat trips.
Leave Stes-Maries by the D38. Within 6km, turn left on to the D85 and cross the Petit Rhône not by bridge but by the flat-bottomed ferry boat, which operates a free shuttle service across the river every ½ hour (if you are in a hurry, then stay on the D38). The D85 is a quiet back road which gives you an even better chance of seeing the Camargue's wildlife. At the D58, turn left for the walled town of Aigues-Mortes.

3 AIGUES-MORTES
Park your car outside the walls and walk through the main gate (still complete with its doors), the Porte de la Gardette. For the best view of the town, which is laid out in an orderly grid pattern, visit the Tour de Constance (Constance Tower) and ramparts.
Le Grau-du-Roi, a bustling little port with a good range of restaurants and gently shelving sandy beach, is along the D979 from Aigues-Mortes. Continue on the coast road to the nearby futuristic resort of La Grande-Motte. Return towards Aigues-Mortes by the inland route, then take the D979 north, turning right on to the N572 for Vauvert and Arles.

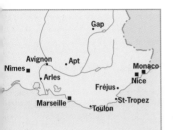

Marseille

Marseille is a big city, but don't be intimidated by the flyovers, factories and urban sprawl on the approach. This is a city which walkers can quite easily get to grips with (after finding a place to park!), for most of the interest lies around the Vieux Port (Old Port). The Vieux Port is Marseille's birthplace and remains its vibrant heart. Belying the images of a dark-alleyed, slightly sinister city riddled with crime, this part of Marseille is colourful – and exceedingly photogenic. See pages 64–5 for the map with route and further details of places mentioned. *Allow a day for the walk.*

From the Office de Tourisme at 4 La Canebière, walk down to quai des Belges.

1 QUAI DES BELGES

Quai des Belges looks out across the Vieux Port, which was discovered by the Phoceans in 600BC. Tiered, pastel-shaded

houses and grand buildings line the quayside, which is the venue for the morning fish market. Overlooking the large harbour, which bristles with a forest of yacht masts, is the enormous neo-Byzantine Basilique de Notre-Dame-de-la-Garde, standing on a 162m-high limestone outcrop.

Quai du Port leads to the handsome Hôtel de Ville, a fine example of 17th-century baroque Provençal architecture. Turn right here along rue de la Prison for the Musée du Vieux Marseille (Museum of Old Marseille) housed in the 16th-century Maison Diamantée. Close by, along rue du Lacydon at place Vivaux, is the Musée des Docks Romains.
Retrace your steps a short way along rue de Lacydon and climb the steps to rue Caisserie, crossing the road to climb a much narrower, historic staircase, montée des Accoules.

2 MONTÉE DES ACCOULES

Montée des Accoules takes you into Le Panier, the oldest part of Marseille. Much of Le Panier was destroyed by the Nazis during the last war. On the hilly slopes above the Vieux Port, the surviving section – a rabbit warren of claustrophobic, narrow streets and alleyways hemmed in by tall buildings – preserves an authentic atmosphere of Marseille as it once was.
Montée des Accoules leads to place de Lenche, where you turn right along rue de l'Évêché, then left along rue Four du Chapitre towards the waterfront and the Cathédrale de la Major. Proceed along avenue Robert Schuman, turning right into rue Antoine-Becker, left along rue de l'Évêché, right into place Francis Chirat,

Fort St-Nicolas is one of two forts (the other is St-Jean) guarding the harbour entrance

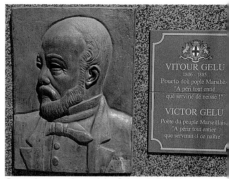

Brass plaque on the quai des Belges dedicated to the Marseille poet Victor Gelu

and right again into rue de l'Observance. The large building on your left is la Vieille Charité (Old Charity Cultural Centre), the entrance to which is off rue de la Charité (turn left at the end of rue de l'Observance). From rue de la Charité turn right into rue Puits du Denier, then left into rue du Panier. Rue des Moulins leads to the pleasant, tree-lined place des Moulins, and on to montée des Accoules. Walk back down the steps, turning left into rue Caisserie, then on to Grand Rue, crossing over rue de la République – one of the city's main streets – to the Jardin des Vestiges (Garden of Ruins).

3 JARDIN DES VESTIGES

You can take a well-earned rest in this attractive sunken garden, excavated to reveal the fortifications of the original Greek town, *Massalia*, 1st-century docks and 3rd-century entranceway. The Musée d'Histoire de Marseille is located here, part of the huge Centre Bourse shopping complex.
From the garden, follow rue Henri Barbusse to rue Reine Élisabeth, turning left into La Canebière for the entrance to the Musée de la Marine et de l'Économie de Marseille.

Nîmes

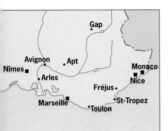

Nîmes has an unexpected variety of faces – part elegant, part shabby, part historic, part futuristic. The ancient heart of the city, a maze of narrow streets and passageways, is ringed by wide and busy roads – boulevard Victor-Hugo, boulevard Gambetta, boulevard de la Libération and boulevard Amiral Courbet. The creation of a conservation zone in 1985 has led to the refurbishment of old Nîmes. Conveniently for those on foot, most of the main sites are concentrated in and around this central area (the beautiful Jardin de la Fontaine, some distance northwest of the centre, is one of the few exceptions). See pages 66–7 for route and details of main sites. *Allow at least half a day for the walk.*

From the Office de Tourisme at 6 rue Auguste, walk a short distance south to the Maison Carrée.

1 MAISON CARRÉE

Along with the Arènes (Roman amphitheatre), this Roman temple is Nîmes's most famous landmark. Across the open space from Maison Carrée lies an architectural counterpoint in the form of a new – and controversial – building of typically bold, uncompromising design. This is the Carré d'Art (Art Cube – tel: 66.76.35.35), the work of British architect Sir Norman Foster. Intended as a Pompidou Centre of the south, it serves as an art gallery and library.
Walk south along boulevard Victor-Hugo, visiting Église St-Paul, built in the 19th century in Romano-Byzantine style. Take rue de la Monnaie to place du Marché.

The Maison Carrée (Square House) was built as a temple in Greek style by the Romans during the reign of Augustus

Place aux Herbes, which contains the former bishop's palace, now a museum

2 PLACE DU MARCHÉ

Place du Marché is the scene of Nîmes's medieval corn market. The charming modern bronze fountain with a crocodile echoes the city's crest.

Leave the place by rue Fresque, a road lined with historic houses. Turn right into rue de Bernis and right again along rue de l'Aspic, a busy shopping street. Turn left into rue de l'Hôtel de Ville. The 15th-century vaulted archway beside the Hôtel de Ville leads to rue de la Trésorerie with the Trésorerie Royale (Royal Treasury) on the right. Turn right into rue Dorée, another street lined with historic but somewhat dilapidated houses. At Grand Rue, turn left.

3 CHAPELLE DES JÉSUITES

The 17th-century former Jesuit Chapel along Grand Rue is one of a number of sites in Nîmes that demonstrate the imaginative, forward-thinking attitude of the city authorities. It is now used for cultural events, and in summer its cool, spacious interior becomes an exhibition area for works of modern art.

Turn left into rue du Chapitre.

4 HÔTEL DE RÉGIS

The Hôtel de Régis at 14 rue du Chapitre is another of the city's many fine old dwellings. An 18th-century façade with a carved entranceway leads into a magnificent cobbled courtyard (16th-century) with Roman artefacts.

Turn right along rue des Marchands for the pretty place aux Herbes and the Cathédrale Notre-Dame et St-Castor, together with its neighbour, the Musée du Vieux Nîmes. Along rue de la Madeleine, take a short detour down rue Ste-Eugénie to see the Église Ste-Eugénie, the oldest church in the city. From rue de la Madeleine, turn left into rue de l'Aspic, which leads south to the Arènes (Roman amphitheatre).

5 ESPLANADE CHARLES DE GAULLE

The Esplanade beyond the Arènes is a pleasant place to end the walk. Its 1848 Fontaine Pradier (named after its sculptor) depicts a female figure who symbolises Nîmes. The grand Palais de Justice (Law Courts), in neoclassical style, stands on one side of the Esplanade.

Var

*T*he Riviera proper starts within this *département*. Away from the main resort areas, the rugged coastlines fringing the forested Massif des Maures and Massif de l'Esterel still preserve their natural beauty. Inland, thickly wooded hills rise into the Haut-Var, a huge expanse of bare plateaux and deserted uplands.

AUPS

At an altitude of over 500m, Aups is traditionally regarded as the beginning of the Alps. Standing among the high plains and empty spaces of the Haut-Var, this peaceful little town preserves an authentic country atmosphere.

Markets are held on Wednesday and Saturday in the square beside the Hôtel de Ville (Town Hall). There is much to appreciate in Aups's unspoilt, leafy old streets: the many fountains, the impressive Renaissance portal and renovated doorway to the Église St-Pancrace, the remains of a town gate and ramparts at the far end of rue des Aires.

Musée Simon Segal

This small gallery displays works by Russian-born painter Simon Segal and other modern artists.

Avenue Albert-1er. Open: daily mid-June to mid-September, 10.30am–noon, 3–6pm. Closed: mid-September to mid-June. Admission charge.

Aups is 29km north of Draguignan.

BANDOL

Bandol has all the attributes of a stylish Côte d'Azur resort: the palm trees, the beaches, the casino, the marina, the expensive villas and condominiums.

The resort has another asset – the Île de Bendor, a short distance offshore, owned by *pastis* magnate Paul Ricard. The small island, accessible by a frequent boat service, contains a diving school, arts and conference centres, and a museum dedicated to wines and spirits.

Sanary-sur-Mer, Bandol's neighbouring resort, also offers boat trips – in this case, to the larger Île des Embiez.

Jardin Exotique et Zoo

This tropical garden and zoo is a popular attraction.

Located near the autoroute exit for Bandol. Tel: 94.29.40.38. Open: 8am–noon, 2–7pm (until dusk in winter). Closed: Sunday morning. Admission charge.

Bandol is about 16km west of Toulon.

One of the many fountains in peaceful Aups, among the hills of the Haut-Var

Bandol, with its marina, casino and elegant villas is the epitome of Côte d'Azur style

VAR

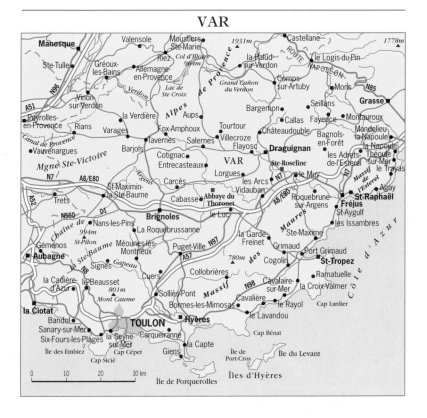

Manosque · Valensole · Moustiers-Ste-Marie · 1931m · Castellane · 1778m

Ste-Tulle · Gréoux-les-Bains · Riez · Col d'Illoire 964m · la Palud-sur-Verdon · le Logis-du-Pin

N96 · Allemagne-en-Provence · Grand Canon du Verdon · Comps-sur-Artuby · Moris · ROUTE NAPOLÉON · N85

Verdon · Lac de Ste Croix · Bargemon · Seillans · Grasse

A51 · Vinon-sur-Verdon · Alpes · Aups · Tourtour · Callas · Fayence · Montauroux

Peyrolles-en-Provence · Rians · la Verdière · Fox-Amphoux · Villecroze · Châteaudouble · Bagnols-en-Forêt · Mandelieu-la-Napoule

Canal de Provence · Varages · Tavernes · Salernes · Flayosq · Draguignan · les Adrets-de-l'Esterel · la Napoule · Théoule-sur-Mer

Vauvenargues · Barjols · Cotignac · Ste-Roseline · Massif de l'Esterel · le Trayas

Mgne Ste-Victoire · Entrecasteaux · VAR · Lorgues · le Muy · Agay

N7 · A8/E80 · Argens · Carcès · les Arcs · N7 · N7 · St-Raphaël

St-Maximin-la-Ste-Baume · Cabasse · Abbaye du Thoronet · Vidauban · A8/E80 · Roquebrune-sur-Argens · Fréjus

Trets · N560 · D1 · le Luc · Maures · St-Aygulf · les Issambres

Chaîne de 994m · Nans-les-Pins · Brignoles · Ste-Maxime · Côte d'Azur

Gémenos · St-Pilon · la Roquebrussanne · la Garde Freinet · Grimaud · Port Grimaud

Aubagne · Méounes-lès-Montrieux · Puget-Ville · N97 · 780m des · Cogolin · St-Tropez

la Ste-Baume · Signes · Gapeau · Collobrières · N98 · Ramatuelle

la Cadière-d'Azur · le Beausset · 801m · Cuers · Massif · Cavalaire-sur-Mer · la Croix-Valmer

Sanary-sur-Mer · Mont Caume · Solliès-Pont · Bormes-les-Mimosas · Cavalière · le Rayol · Cap Lardier

la Ciotat · Bandol · TOULON · Hyères · le Lavandou

Six-Fours-les-Plages · la Seyne-sur-Mer · Carqueiranne · Cap Bénat

Île des Embiez · Cap Cépet · Giens · la Capte · Île de Port-Cros · Île du Levant

Cap Sicié · 0 10 20 30 km · Île de Porquerolles · Îles d'Hyères

BORMES-LES-MIMOSAS

You can forgive the locals for embellishing the name of this hilltop village, originally known simply as Bormes. They have made sure that Bormes – rechristened Bormes-les-Mimosas in 1968 – earns its name. There are flowers everywhere, in baskets, urns, tubs, pots and window boxes, climbing up the fronts of the houses, and in immaculately tended flowerbeds.

The part of Bormes that attracts visitors – the Vieux Village (Old Village) – is perched at the top of a steep, south-facing slope, with wonderful views of nearby Le Lavandou and the coast. The alleyways and narrow streets can be explored by following a waymarked *Circuit Touristique* with numbered stopping-off places (details from the tourist office, SEMIBO-Service Tourisme, tel: 94.71.15.17/94.71.17.07). Bormes is almost too perfect: the street names are a little fanciful – montée du Paradis, for instance – and there are even special slatted cubbyholes in which to hide the dustbins!

Musée d'Art et Histoire

Bormes's history together with the work of local artist Jean-Charles Cazin (1841–1901) are the main themes here. *65 rue Carnot. Tel: 94.71.15.08. Open: July to September, Wednesday to Sunday, 10am–noon, 4–6pm (except Sunday afternoon); remainder of year, Wednesday 10am–noon, 3–5pm, Sunday 10am–noon. Admission charge.*

Bormes-les-Mimosas is off the D559 about 22km east of Hyères.

DRAGUIGNAN

This large town stands at the gateway to the high country of the Haut-Var. There is not a great deal to distract visitors passing through on the way to the Grand Cañon du Verdon. The most attractive part of the town is the medieval quarter around the place du Marché, the Tour de l'Horloge (a fine 17th-century clock tower) and the Église St-Michel, guarded by ancient gateways.

Bormes-les-Mimosas: picture postcard perfection for the tourists

Musée des Arts et Traditions Populaires

Exhibits include traditional costumes, agricultural implements and a Provençal kitchen.

15 rue Joseph-Roumanille. Tel: 94.47.05.72. Open: 9am–noon, 2–6pm. Closed Sunday morning and all day Monday. Admission charge.

Draguignan is 30km northwest of Fréjus.

FRÉJUS/ST RAPHAËL

Fréjus is a place of many parts, and blends into its more fashionable neighbour, St-Raphaël. Most visitors come for the beach, Fréjus-Plage, at the western end of this sprawling coastal town. In the east there is a swish new marina and harbour complex, while beyond that a long, sandy beach ends at St-Raphaël's attractive harbour and seafront casino.

The town of Fréjus itself, a kilometre or so inland, is noted for its Roman remains. *Forum Julii* was an impressively large Roman town and port: too large, perhaps, for us to appreciate fully today, since vestiges of Roman occupation are scattered across a wide area, making it difficult to build up any coherent picture. Beside the N7 into town from the northeast are ruined arches from a 40km aqueduct system. An open-air theatre (still used for concerts) stands incongruously amongst quiet suburbs along avenue du Théâtre-Romain, while the Arènes (amphitheatre) lies beyond the Porte des Gaules gateway in the west of the town.

Medieval Fréjus's centrepiece is the Cathedral Close, a collection of important religious buildings dating back to early Christian times.

A slice of Provençal life in Draguignan's Museum of Popular Arts and Traditions

Arènes (Amphitheatre)

Although not as impressive as others in Provence, it is still used for concerts and bullfights.

Rue Henri-Vadon. Tel: 94.51.34.31. Open: April to September, 9.30am–noon, 2–6pm; October to March, 9am–noon, 2–4.30pm. Closed: Tuesday. Admission charge.

Cathedral Close

The well-preserved baptistery here is one of the oldest in France. It stands next to an impressive 10th- to 13th-century cathedral built in an austere early Provençal style. Lighter in effect are its slender-columned cloisters, enclosing a delightful little garden. An archaeological museum is also located here.

Place Formigé. Tel: 94.51.26.30. Cathedral open in the mornings and 4–6pm. Free. Baptistery, cloisters and museum open April to September, daily 9am–7pm; October to March, 9am–noon, 2–5pm. Closed: Tuesdays in October to March. Admission charge.

HYÈRES

Miraculously, the town of Hyères has avoided the worse excesses of Côte tourism, possibly because of its location a short distance inland (the coast has receded since medieval times, when Hyères served as a port for the Crusades). Even the 'new' Hyères of the 19th century, which covers the hill on the approach to the old town, has preserved its original decorum. This area, with its wide streets, waving palm trees, gardens, grand villas and casino, retains the character of its *belle époque* when it rivalled Nice as a fashionable resort for the rich and famous (Queen Victoria stayed here once).

The Vieille Ville of medieval Hyères lies beyond the ancient gateway at place Georges-Clémenceau. Suddenly, you are amongst the narrow, typically claustro-phobic streets of a *real* French town in which real people live and work. Old Hyères has not been cosmeticised with overly pretty features and overtly expensive shops – and is all the more refreshing for it. Place Massillon, venue of a daily market, is a delightful little self-

Popular since the 19th century, Hyères is more of a genuine town than many other resorts

contained Provençal square surrounded by tall buildings and unglamorous cafés. It is overlooked by the Tour St-Blaise, a 12th-century tower of the Knights Templar.

The Vieille Ville's main church, the imposing 13th-century Église St-Louis, is on place de la République east of place Massillon. Hyères's most memorable religious site stands high on the hill in place St-Paul. Collégiale St-Paul is a former collegiate church attached by archway to a Renaissance house with a fairytale conical turret (the Romanesque church is open afternoons, except Monday). Place St-Paul, a magnificent viewpoint 5km from the sea, looks out past the narrow spit of land known as Presqu'île de Giens to the Îles d'Hyères. If you have the energy, you can climb yet further up the hill to the flower-filled Parc St-Bernard and a ruined château. *Hyères's beaches lie to the south, along Hyères-Plage and the 5km-long Presqu'île de Giens.*

Jardin Olbius-Riquier

This attractive garden, south of the town, contains a lake, children's play area, aviaries, a profusion of exotic plants and a small zoo.
Avenue Ambroise-Thomas. Open: daily 7.30am–dusk. Free.

Musée Municipal

Greek and Roman finds from local excavations are on display, together with paintings and items of natural history *Place Lefèbvre. Tel: 94.65.12.07. Open: 10am–noon, 3–6pm. Closed: Saturday and Sunday afternoon and all day Tuesday. Admission charge.*

ÎLES D'HYÈRES

Boats for the islands of Porquerolles, Port-Cros and Le Levant – also known as the Îles d'Or (Golden Isles) – depart daily all year round from Port d'Hyères, next to Hyères-Plage. A few kilometres east of Hyères, La Londe-les-Maures/Port-de-Miramar has daily boat trips from mid-June to mid-September. One-way journeys last from 30–90 minutes depending on port of departure, with shorter times from La Londe. (Further details from the Office de Tourisme, Rotonde Jean Salusse, avenue de Belgique, BP 721, 83412 Hyères Cedex; tel: 94.65.18.55.)

The nearest and largest of these islands, Porquerolles, is predictably the most developed, though everything is on a small scale. From its village you can walk or cycle (bikes can be rented locally) through a landscape of pine trees, eucalyptus and heather to some beautiful sandy beaches and stunning stretches of cliff scenery. There is a small museum in Fort Ste-Agathe, a stronghold overlooking the village.

The Île de Port-Cros, more or less uninhabited, is a thickly vegetated haven that supports a wealth of wildlife. The smallest national park in France, this is the place to go for those interested in natural history. The Île du Levant, the furthest of the three islands from Hyères, is mainly a military base.

LE LAVANDOU

Travelling eastwards along the coast, you will begin to sense the presence of first-division glamour – and serious money – on reaching Le Lavandou. This is another fishing village that has become a glittering haven for holiday yachts. Not as densely developed as many of its contemporaries, it boasts a fine, spacious sandy beach and an animated harbour. Boats leave from the harbour for the Îles d'Hyères. The coast road east winds its way along the mountain-backed Corniche des Maures to St-Tropez.
Le Lavandou is 23km east of Hyères.

Sea, sand and sunshine at Le Lavandou – but expect high prices in the town

THE JET SET

The Riviera has long been a playground of the wealthy, the very name conjuring up images of 24-carat lifestyles involving luxury yachts, palatial hotels, bougainvillaea-draped villas, private beaches and spinning roulette wheels.

DISCOVERING THE RIVIERA

It was not always so. When the English novelist Tobias Smollett sought a cure for his bronchitis in Nice in 1764, he wrote of a land of 'rude peasants and persistent mosquitoes', though he did find the climate to his taste. Another Englishman, Lord Brougham – the Lord Chancellor, no less – found it even more to his liking 90 years later, when an enforced stay in the tiny fishing village of Cannes proved far more agreeable than he had expected. Within a decade, so many of his compatriots were travelling south for the winter that Nice had a Promenade des Anglais (Promenade of the English). By the end of the 19th century, the Riviera was playing host to Queen Victoria and the crowned heads of Italy, Sweden, Bulgaria and Belgium, as well as Grand Dukes of Russia and the Shah of Persia. 'Princes, princes, nothing but princes,' grumbled that master of the short story, Guy de Maupassant.

THE SHOW GOES ON

The clientele changed with the social upheaval that followed World War I. Newly rich Americans swarmed in with their taste for high living, making the Riviera a symbol of the Jazz Age. It was here that Gabrielle 'Coco' Chanel – perfumer and fashion designer – made sunbathing chic, and nowhere did the Roaring Twenties roar more excitingly. In the 1930s, the Duke of Windsor – who abdicated rather than give up the divorced Wallis Simpson – even thought of marrying on the Riviera. The area's seal of

Antibes (above) and St Tropez are the
playgrounds of the seriously rich

fashionable approval was again
renewed when film star Grace Kelly
came here to marry Prince Rainier.

Today the Côte d'Azur is as siren-
like as ever, despite the dangers of
being swamped by its own success.
Movie stars, millionaires, pop singers,
successful writers – all fall victim to the
allure of sunshine, sybaritic living and
the prestige that comes with being one
of the jet set. And the myth touches

millions. If mere mortals can afford the
price of a meal in one of St-Tropez's
best restaurants, or a room in the
Carlton at Cannes, then they join,
however briefly, the exclusive ranks of
the seriously rich and famous.

You have to go a few kilometres south from St Tropez to enjoy the beaches

ST-TROPEZ

There are those who say that St-Tropez is impossible and over-hyped. And they are probably correct if they are referring to the resort in high summer. But come in the quieter months, and you immediately appreciate why St-Tropez has cast a spell over so many, from Matisse to Brigitte Bardot.

After such heightened expectations, St-Tropez's diminutive size comes as quite a surprise. The Vieux Port (Old Port) is the heart of St-Tropez. It is here that the multi-millionaires moor their huge yachts. It is here that the merely rich come to parade. And it is here that the *petit bourgeois* come to gawp at the ostentatious displays of wealth.

Behind the Vieux Port lies a picturesque town and the rue de la Citadelle, which leads to a high bluff dominated by a mighty 16th-century fortress.

St-Tropez's beach area lies a few kilometres to the south. The Plage de Pampellone, although offering 5km of sand, becomes exceedingly busy in summer. Further south again, around Cape Camarat, there is a better chance of finding a quieter spot along the Plage de l'Escalet.

At the approach to the St-Tropez Peninsula is Port Grimaud. Reclaimed from marshland in the 1960s, it is a mostly successful attempt to create the look of a traditional fishing village in the modern idiom. Inland is the pretty hilltop village of Grimaud, capped by a ruined château.

La Citadelle et Musée Naval

The 16th-century fort is now a naval museum reflecting St-Tropez's maritime history.

Tel: 94.97 06.53. Open: Wednesday to Monday, summer 10am–6pm; winter (except November) 10am–5pm. Closed: November. Admission charge.

Cannons guard the 16th-century tower housing Ste-Maxime's local museum

Musée de l'Annonciade

This outstanding gallery contains the best selection of 1890–1950 paintings outside Paris: Braque, Dufy, Matisse, Signac, Utrillo and many others.
Place Grammont. Tel: 94.97.04.01. Open: Wednesday to Monday, June to September, 10am–noon, 4–8pm; October to May, 10am–noon, 2–6pm. Closed: November. Admission charge.

STE-MAXIME

Ste-Maxime, across the bay from St-Tropez, is an attractive, unpretentious resort. The seafront Office de Tourisme has a fascinating display of postcards depicting the Ste-Maxime of old.

Musée des Traditions Locales

Items of local folklore and traditions are housed in a 16th-century tower.
Tour Carrée. Tel: 94.96.70.30. Open: Monday to Saturday, 10am–noon, 2–4pm. Closed: November. Admission charge.

TOULON

Capital of the Var and France's second-largest naval base, Toulon merits at least a mention in any guidebook to Provence. But it is mainly a large, modern and undistinguished city, with the exception

of parts of the Vieille Ville (Old Town) behind quai Stalingrad and quai de la Sinse, an area that escaped the relentless bombings of World War II. North of the city, a cablecar climbs to the summit of Mont Faron, from which you can appreciate Toulon's maritime appeal as a perfectly sheltered, capacious harbour.

Musée Naval

Toulon's long-standing associations with the sea are explained through model ships, drawings and *memorabilia*.
Place Monsenergue. Tel: 94.02.02.01. Open: 10am–noon, 1.30–6pm. Closed: Tuesday. Admission charge.

Musée de Toulon/d'Histoire Naturelle

The former contains an excellent collection of paintings and sculptures, works from Breughel to Francis Bacon.
113 boulevard Général-Leclerc. Tel: 94.93.15.54. Musée de Toulon open: daily 1–7pm. Musée d'Histoire Naturelle open: Monday to Saturday, 9.30am–noon, 2–6pm; Sunday 1–7pm. Admission is free to both.

The naval base of Toulon has one of the finest natural harbours in France

L'Esterel

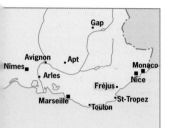

The Massif de l'Esterel, a mountain range which rises to over 600m, is the perfect antidote to the Côte d'Azur's curse of too many people and too much development. This wild, rugged and largely impenetrable upland, covered in *maquis* (scrub), a dense covering of heathers, gorse, mimosa, lavender and other shrubs, has a coastal equivalent along the indented Corniche de l'Esterel. Although just a stone's throw from Cannes, this is the least built-up stretch of coastline between Toulon and the Italian border, though how long it will remain so is open to question. On this tour, you will see a rash of new development, some of it clinging precariously to impossibly steep slopes in order to achieve that all-important sea view. *Allow a full day, including some time to stop off at the coast.*

From Fréjus, take the coast road via the marina to St-Raphaël (see page 83). On leaving St-Raphaël by the N98 coast road you will

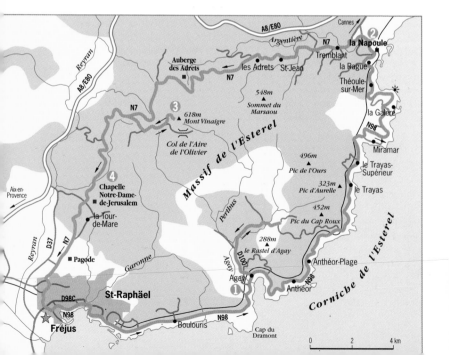

soon be amongst the rich red volcanic rocks, small coves and sand-and-pebble beaches that characterise the Corniche de l'Esterel (its nickname is the Corniche d'Or, the 'Golden Corniche'). On the approach to Agay, there are excellent views of craggy, burnished mountains tumbling down into open seas.

1 AGAY

Agay is the only resort of any significant size on the Corniche, and a refreshing change from the pseudo-sophistication of some of its better-known sister resorts. Its attractive beach and small harbour lie snugly within a sheltered horseshoe-shaped bay.

From Agay you can take a detour inland, initially along the D100, and then turning right after a few kilometres along a twisting road through the hills for the superb viewpoints of the Pic du Cap Roux (452m), the Pic d'Aurelle (323m) and the Pic de l'Ours (496m).

The coast road from Agay leads to the smaller seaside centre of Anthéor and Anthéor-Plage (Beach). Le Trayas, just before Miramar, is the highest point on the Corniche. The road overlooks a rugged section of coastline, though there is an abrupt change of scene on the approach to Théoule-sur-Mer when Cannes and the densely developed Golfe de Napoule come into view.

2 LA NAPOULE

The small resort of La Napoule, with its large, boat-filled harbour, marks the start of the Riviera proper. Its château, dating from the 14th century, was much altered by American sculptor Henry Clews at the start of this century. Critics call it a tasteless folly. See if you agree by taking a guided tour (available afternoons March to October except Tuesday – tel: 93.49.95.05).

For the return leg of the tour, follow the N7 inland, a scenic road that skirts the northern slopes of the Massif de l'Esterel, following mainly the Roman route Via Aurelia. The Auberge des Andrets was the haunt of a highwayman in the 18th century. About 5km after the Auberge, turn left for Mont Vinaigre.

3 MONT VINAIGRE

Mont Vinaigre, at 618m, is the highest point in the Massif (there are also spectacular views from the Col de l'Aire de l'Olivier just to the south). This is excellent walking country, with a good network of trails and picnic areas. Its single chamber is brightly decorated with murals.

Return to the N7, a road that twists and turns on the descent to Fréjus.

4 CHAPELLE NOTRE-DAME-DE-JÉRUSALEM

Stop off at this chapel. Its single chamber is brightly decorated with murals by Jean Cocteau. Further along the road a few kilometres from your return to Fréjus is a Vietnamese pagoda, used as a Buddhist temple.

Wild boar roam the forests of the Esterel Massif rising behind the Côte d'Azur

Alpes-Maritimes

*T*he busiest stretch of the Côte d'Azur – including the tiny independent Principality of Monaco – lies between Cannes and the Italian border. This is the Riviera at its most incandescent and infuriating. The contrast between coast and country could not be more striking. Within an hour's drive of the Mediterranean is a *département* of hidden valleys, remote, inaccessible uplands and wild Alpine scenery.

ANTIBES

The Cap d'Antibes promontory jutting out into the Mediterranean between Cannes and Nice is made up of two fashionable resorts, Antibes and Juan-les-Pins (see page 102). Antibes, on the eastern shore, is a honeypot for celebrities and the seriously rich. The millionaires in search of more privacy hide themselves away behind high fences in their exclusive mansions around Cap d'Antibes.

Antibes also attracts artists. Picasso's studio was at Château Grimaldi, an unmissable landmark on the headland above the old town. The medieval château and stout sea wall guard Antibes's characterful old quarter, by far more enticing than the busy, bland modern town further inland. Look out among the narrow streets for the cathedral (noted for its magnificent early 18th-century doors) and

unapologetically workaday covered market. The Vieux Port (Old Port) has been completely overshadowed by the massive modern harbour of neighbouring Port Vauban – mooring place of some of Europe's most fabulous yachts – overlooked by the 16th-century Fort Carré.

Musée d'Archéologie
Antibes has a long history. This museum tells the story of Etruscan, Greek, Roman and medieval settlement here. *Bastion St-André. Tel: 93.34.48.01. Open: Wednesday to Monday, summer, 9am–noon, 3–7pm; winter, 9am–noon, 2–6pm. Closed: November. Admission charge.*

Musée Picasso
Picasso worked 'like a madman' for the six months he spent at Château Grimaldi after World War II.

Picasso in the Musée Picasso

From July to December 1946 his work achieved new heights of creative genius. His gift to Antibes for the use of the château was the artistic output of his stay. This outstanding collection forms the basis of the Picasso Museum, which was later enriched by further works of his (tapestries, engravings and lithographs) together with paintings and sculptures from many other leading artists such as Miró, Modigliani, Léger and Ernst, and photographs of Picasso by Bill Brandt and Man Ray.

Château Grimaldi, place Marijol. Tel: 93.34.91.91. Open: see Musée d'Archéologie for details. Admission charge.

ALPES-MARITIMES

BIOT

The bond between Vallauris and Picasso (see page 116) is mirrored by Biot's strong links with Fernand Léger (1881–1955). The inland village, north of Antibes, was Léger's home for the last few years of his life, and is the location of an important museum dedicated to the artist.

The medieval village, well known for its pottery and glassware (bubble glass is the local speciality), is a mixture of gateways, narrow lanes and sloping streets. Most visitors make for the rue St-Sébastien, where the potteries and glass shops are concentrated. You can see glassblowers at work in the Verrerie de Biot on chemin des Combes; the shop is on rue St-Sébastien.

Musée d'Histoire Locale

A restored kitchen is one of the exhibits in this museum of local life.
Place de la Chapelle. Tel: 93.65.11.79 or 93.65.05.85. Open: Tuesday to Sunday,

The narrow streets of medieval Biot are full of craft studios and shops

April to September, 2.30–5.30pm; November to March, Thursday, Saturday and Sunday 2.30–6pm. Closed: October. Admission charge.

Musée National Fernand Léger

A complete cross-section of the artist's work is on display, from early post-Cubism to the more direct man-and-industry canvases of his later period.
Off the D4 southeast of the village. Tel: 93.65.63.49 or 93.65.63.61. Open: Wednesday to Monday 10am–noon, 2–6pm (until 5pm November to March). Admission charge.

Biot is on the D4, accessible off the N7, in the hills north of Antibes.

CAGNES-SUR-MER

The best part of ungainly, sprawling Cagnes-sur-Mer is Haut-de-Cagnes, the old medieval quarter set high on a ridge overlooking the coast. Here, you will find the usual 'perched village' picture of perfection: an ancient château (now a museum-cum-art gallery), exquisite

SOPHIA-ANTIPOLIS

When you drive between Nice and Cannes, you will see frequent signs to Sophia-Antipolis, a place few visitors will be familiar with. Sophia-Antipolis, a vast science and technology park, points the way in which the Côte d'Azur is heading.

By the 21st century, the Riviera's high-tech enterprises will well and truly have eclipsed old-fashioned tourism. The park, which pairs the Greek word for wisdom with the name of their ancient settlement at nearby Antibes, is a complete purpose-built town with its own shops and facilities. The European equivalent to California's Silicon Valley, Sophia-Antipolis unashamedly exploits the 'feel-good' factor. What better place to attract a contented, quality workforce than a landscaped site with blissful weather and every possible amenity, all close to Nice's international airport?

Sophia-Antipolis's 'sun, silicon and software' package has proved irresistible. Hundreds of companies are now located here, including Air France, IBM and the Digital Equipment Corporation.

These panels illustrate Biot's modern artistic legacy: the art of Fernand Léger

homes and expensive restaurants, on a wooded outcrop prettified by sweet-scented ornamental gardens.

Back along the coast, Cagnes is famous for its racecourse-by-the-sea and associations with Auguste Renoir (1841–1919).

Musée Renoir

Parts of the house in which Renoir spent the last 11 years of his life look as if the artist is still at work.

La Maison de Renoir, Les Collettes. Tel: 93.20.61.07. Open: Wednesday to Monday, June to mid-October, 10am–noon, 2–6pm; mid-November to May, 2–5pm. Admission charge.

Cagnes-sur-Mer is between Nice and Antibes.

Cannes

*C*annes is big, busy and, amazingly enough, still beautiful in parts. In 1834 the English Lord Chancellor, Lord Brougham, arrived here after fleeing from cholera-stricken Nice. He liked what he saw, built a villa and – *voilà!* – the resort was born. Constant redevelopment continues apace on this febrile stretch of coast: the Cannes of today is not even a resort in the usual sense, more a year-round meeting place for businessmen, conference delegates and, of course, film stars.

The hub of modern Cannes is the Palais des Festivals, the vast convention centre overlooking the Vieux Port (Old Port). This great lump of a building, opened in 1982, illustrates where the priorities of the town planners lie. Everything is laid on with maximum convenience for the delegates. The immaculately tended main beaches are to the right and left, while the seafront boulevard de la Croisetteis but a stone's throw away (the Carlton's sculpted, gleaming white façade really does look like a piece of wedding cake).

To return to reality, you have to climb the hill into Le Suquet, the old

quarter on the western side of the port. Founded by the Romans, it later became the property of the monks of the Îles de Lérins a short distance offshore. Tour Le Suquet, the 11th-century watchtower crowning the summit, is a magnificent viewpoint. The tower shares the hilltop with the Musée de la Castre and the Gothic-style Église Notre-Dame d'Espérance, completed in 1648.

If you are on a budget, then the restaurants in Le Suquet's narrow streets are your best bet for eating out. Back in the main town, rue d'Antibes and rue Meynadier are Cannes's fashionable shopping thoroughfares, though for more down-to-earth produce there is the covered market, the Marché Forville.

The quietest side of Cannes is at La Croisette at the far end of the seafront boulevard. But if you really want to get away from it all, then take the 15-minute boat trip from the Vieux Port to the tranquil islands known collectively as the Îles de Lérins: St-Honorat, with its monastic associations, and the larger Ste-Marguerite.

Mougins, a short distance inland from Cannes, is a delightful perched village of expensive restaurants and exclusive shops. It stands on a 260m-high outcrop, insulated from the busy world at its feet.

Modern art in a Cannes street

The new Cannes of conference centres is taking over from the old seaside resort

from many countries and cultures – Mediterranean, Egyptian, Far Eastern, South American, etc. There is also a permanent exhibition of Provençal landscapes.

Le Suquet. Tel: 93.38.55.26. Open: Wednesday to Monday, July to September, 10am–noon, 3–7pm; April to June, 10am–noon, 2–6pm; October to March, 10am–noon, 2–5pm. Admission charge.

Chapelle Bellini

The painter Emmanuel Bellini used this Florentine-baroque-style chapel, built in 1880, for his studio.

Parc Fiorentina, 67 bis, avenue de Vallauris. Tel: 93.39.15.55. Open: 2–5pm or by appointment. Admission charge.

Musée de la Castre

Located in the old citadel at the top of the hill, the museum contains antiquities

Musée de la Mer (Museum of the Sea)

This museum is within the fort on the island of Ste-Marguerite. Not just maritime in theme, its exhibits include items from local shipwrecks, artefacts excavated on the island, and the rooms of the old state prison at the fort, including the cell of the fabled Man in the Iron Mask.

Île Ste-Marguerite. Tel: 93.68.91.92 or 93.38.55.26. Open: Wednesday to Monday, July to September, 10.30am–noon, 2–6.30pm; April to June, 10.30am–noon, 2–5.30pm; October to March, 10.30am–noon, 2–4.30pm. Admission charge.

CANNES FILM FESTIVAL

There is only one place for the world's film-makers to be in May – Cannes, home of the International Film Festival. For two weeks the resort swarms with producers, directors, stars, starlets, minders, has-beens, hangers-on, deal-makers, journalists, moguls and would-be moguls. Deals are struck by hotel pools or in expensive restaurants in an atmosphere as unreal as anything created on a Hollywood set, the only certainty being that at the end of it all the resort of Cannes ends up a good deal wealthier.

BORN OF RIVALRY

Curiously, all this hype and hysteria would never have come about at all had it not been for Benito Mussolini. The Italian dictator inaugurated the Venice Film Festival in the mid-1930s. The French, in retaliation for the fact that all the major prizes went to Fascist-oriented films, devised a rival festival. Their timing was less than serendipitous: set for a launch in September 1939, the festival was postponed until 1947 owing to the outbreak of war.

The new festival was not an overnight success. It was still small enough in the 1950s for all those involved to be put aboard a small motor boat for a lunch on the nearby Île Ste-Marguerite. But change was in the air. In the mid-'50s, Brigitte Bardot made a huge impact at Cannes, and by the end

of the decade American influence – and money – transformed the festival into a frenetic event characterised by wheeling and dealing, unbridled excess and controlled chaos.

COMING OF AGE

Cannes in the 1960s became Hollywood's shop window in Europe, and as the TV industry expanded worldwide, followed by video, satellite and cable, the scale of the festival increased dramatically. Today, about 50,000 people descend on Cannes each year. A few of them, if they can find the time, might even watch a movie or two during their stay. The best film is awarded the Palme d'Or, the highest accolade in the film world after the almighty Oscar.

A glittering array of stars attends Cannes '94 (below and bottom)

... and woman was created – Brigitte Bardot

The panorama from Eze's Jardins Exotique, at the summit of this precipitous village

Its chief glory is an unusual Catalan crucifix of the mid-13th century which depicts a smiling Christ.

Jardin Exotique

This unusual garden of cacti and succulents is located amongst the ruins of Eze's castle.
Tel: 93.41.10.30 or 93.41.03.03. Open: daily, summer 9am–8pm; winter 9am–dusk. Admission charge.

Eze is between Monaco and Nice.

GOURDON

Spectacularly located, Gourdon is another sheer-sided perched village. Although there are one or two classy shops selling perfume and soap, it is best to ignore the tacky tourist knick-knacks and concentrate instead on the castle and magnificent view southwards to the coast.

Château de Gourdon

The immaculately restored 13th-century castle has an excellent display of arms and armour, and an interesting art collection.
Tel: 93.42.50.13. Open: Wednesday to Monday, June to September, 11am–noon, 2–7pm; October to May, daily (except Tuesday), 10am–noon, 2–6pm. Admission charge.

Gourdon is on the D3, 14km northeast of Grasse.

GRASSE

This charming town, set in shallow but sheltering hill country less than 20km from the coast, has a graceful, calming

EZE

Of all the perched villages inland from the coast, Eze is the most dramatic. It is not so much perched as precariously balanced on a jagged, precipitous outcrop. The easiest approach is along the N7 – you can, if you are lucky, find a space in the car park at the foot of the village and then walk up into the maze of narrow vaulted passageways, crooked steps and secretive corners. Inevitably, it is nowadays almost entirely a tourist village of galleries, restaurants and shops, yet they fail to eclipse Eze's breathtaking setting 470m above sea level, and the integrity of its restored medieval architecture.

Paradoxically, its strongest point – the original castle – has suffered most from the ravages of time. The 14th-century Chapelle des Pénitents Blancs on place du Planet is in rather better condition.

Not just a pretty face, she tells you the time (but only up to 3 o'clock): sun dial in Gourdon

Musée International de la Parfumerie

The museum deals with the history and manufacture of perfume.

8 place du Cours. Tel: 93.36.01.61. Open: daily, June to September, 10am–7pm; October to May, Wednesday to Sunday, 10am–noon, 2–5pm. Admission charge.

Villa-Musée Fragonard

Works by Fragonard can be seen in this 18th-century villa in which the artist lived. The Parfumerie Fragonard, at 20 boulevard Fragonard, is a museum of perfume (admission free).

23 boulevard Fragonard. Tel: 93.40.32.64. Open: daily, June to September, 10am–1pm, 2p–pm; October to May, Wednesday to Sunday, 10am–noon, 2–7pm. Admission charge.

Fountain and flowers adorn sweet-smelling Grasse's place aux Aires

air. Its surrounding meadowlands yield the fragrant flowers that have made Grasse famous as a perfume town. Whenever you visit you will be assailed by fragrance: mimosas in spring, roses and lavender in summer, jasmine in autumn. The town has not been able to distance itself completely from the overdevelopment along the coast. But although Grasse has its modern housing and high-technology parks, it is still an appealing mixture of the handsome and the humble: fine old buildings and traditional workaday shopping streets.

These two contrasting sides to Grasse are closest together along the elegant terraced gardens in front of the grand Palais des Congrès. Take the steps down into rue Jean-Ossola and you are immediately enclosed within an old town of narrow streets. A daily market is held at place aux Aires, while place du Petit-Puy is the site of Grasse's cathedral, dating from the 12th century.

It is well worth devoting some time to this part of Grasse and its museums, despite the towns overwhelming association with perfume (see box on page 102). There are around 30 major *parfumeries* in and around the town (ask at the Office de Tourisme, Palais des Congrès, for details – tel: 93.36.66.66).

ISOLA 2000

This is one for the skiing enthusiasts. Despite the fact that it is one of the southernmost Alpine resorts and only 1½ hours from Nice, Isola has a good snow record. If you are familiar with other French Alpine resorts, then Isola will hold no surprises. The functional approach, devoid of any Alpine charm, does at least deliver super-convenient doorstep skiing. Its unimaginative name derives from its altitude.

The resort, accessible by the tortuous D2205 through the Gorges of the Tinée, is only a few kilometres from the Italian border. Its proximity to the Parc National du Mercantour (see pages 138–9) gives some credence to its claim of being a year-round resort, especially since accommodation costs are much lower in the summer 'off-season'.

Further along the Tinée Valley is Auron, the oldest ski-resort in the Alpes-Maritimes.

JUAN-LES-PINS

Juan-les-Pins is *the* place to be seen at night on the exclusive peninsula of Cap d'Antibes (see also Antibes, page 92). By day, you wonder what all the fuss is about, for Juan-les-Pins is an unexceptional little resort, neat and tidy but disappointingly bland. It wakes up after the sun goes down, when the clubs, bars and restaurants attract the Cap's well-heeled villa owners and glamour-seekers. F Scott Fitzgerald, aided and abetted by a few rich fellow

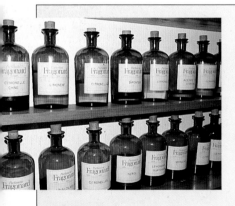

PERFUME

Flower-filled Provence is the most aromatic part of France. The most fragrant corner of all is Grasse, a town that makes its living by bottling the scents of southern France.

Grasse's perfume industry began in the 16th century when immigrant Italian glovemakers decided to scent their leather gloves with perfume made from the local flowers. Over the next few hundred years, an entire industry developed in Grasse based on its floral perfumes. Nowadays, around 30 major *parfumeries* are based in and around the town, using a mixture of imported and local materials to make perfumes, many of which are sold under brand names such as Dior and Estée Lauder.

Huge quantities of floral material go into the creation of the highly concentrated essences known as essential oils or absolutes. The art of the perfumer lies in the blending of these essential oils and other ingredients, a complex process that results in the creation of a particular fragrance.

Many of Grasse's *parfumeries* welcome visitors, and there are museums in the town that explain the history and manufacture of perfume (see page 101).

Beach addicts enjoy Juan-les-Pins by day, but after sundown is when it really wakes up

Americans, colonised this stretch of coast in the 1920s, creating the fabulous myth that Juan-les-Pins has been living off ever since. Part of Fitzgerald's novel *Tender Is the Night* is set here, and he wrote to a friend, 'I'd like to live and die on the French Riviera.'

Musée Naval et Napoléonien
Model ships are displayed, along with items relating to Napoleon's return from exile on Elba and other *memorabilia*. *Batterie du Grillon, boulevard John-F-Kennedy (at Cap d'Antibes south of Juan-les-Pins). Tel: 93.61.45.32. Open: Monday to Friday, 9.30am–noon, 2.15–6pm; Saturday 9.30am–noon. Closed: October. Admission charge.*

Juan-les-Pins is a few kilometres from Antibes, on the opposite side of the Cap d'Antibes peninsula.

Menton

'*Ma ville est un jardin*' ('My town is a garden'), claims the tourist literature for Menton – and for once it is right. Menton, almost within shouting distance of the Italian border, is the French Riviera's floral town *par excellence*. Its exceptional sunshine record, coupled with a subtropical climate and a patently garden-mad town council, have conspired to produce a resort bursting with colourful floral beds, luscious orange, lemon and palm trees, and beautiful award-winning areas of greenery. Where else would you find a place that holds a Fête du Citron in February, a festival of floats and tableaux made entirely of flowers, oranges and, of course, lemons?

Menton, unlike its more illustrious neighbours, has not embraced the growth-at-any-cost philosophy. Consequently, it is still a true resort as opposed to a conurbation by the sea. The Vieille Ville (Old Town), a cluster of pastel-shaded houses riddled with steep alleyways, has an almost Italianate air. All passageways eventually lead to place de la Conception on the highest ground

Prettily packaged local herbs make good gifts

above the Vieux Port (Old Port) and two ornate religious sites – the Église de la Conception and the Église St-Michel.

The sturdy fortified building on quai Napoléon pays homage to Jean Cocteau, though fans of the artist will also want to see the way he transformed the humble Salle des Mariages (registry office) in the Hôtel de Ville (Town Hall) in 1957.

West of quai Napoléon along baie du Soleil lies Menton's main beach. The promenade – and, for that matter, the entire resort – has an unexpectedly genteel, relaxed air, due in no small part to its popularity with elderly retired folk attracted by Menton's calm, sunny climate. The lucky ones are able to afford the villas in the hilly Garavan district east of the Vieux Port, a gorgeous garden suburb thick with exotic vegetation and blessed with marvellous sea views. Avenue Katherine-Mansfield, named after the writer who had a retreat here, winds its way through this privileged quarter. Here you will also find the Jardin des Colombières, the best in the Garavan district and one of the finest on the Riviera.

Jardin des Colombières

Created by writer and artist Ferdinand Bac, the hilltop Jardin des Colombières,

Popular since the 19th century, picturesque Menton climbs up from its harbour

with its fountains, statuary, balustrades, ornamental pools, cypresses and sea views, is the ultimate romantic Riviera garden.
Boulevard de Garavan. Tel: 93.35.71.90. Open: daily 10am–noon, 2–6pm. Admission charge.

Musée Cocteau
Cocteau's paintings are beautifully presented in this 17th-century bastion. The painter and poet, who lived locally, designed the mosaic floor and donated many works of art.
Bastion du Vieux Port, quai Napoléon III. Tel: 93.57.72.30. Open: Wednesday to Monday, mid-June to mid-September, 10am–noon, 3–7pm; mid-September to mid-June, 10am–noon, 2–6pm. Free.

Musée de la Préhistoire Régionale
The star attraction at this museum is the famous 'Menton Man', a 30,000-year-old skull. Local traditions and culture are also covered.
Rue Lorédan-Larchey. Tel: 93.35.84.64. Open: see Musée Cocteau for details. Free.

Place de la Conception
The dominant building here is the baroque Église St-Michel, pink and ochre outside and ornate within. The sunken square just outside is the venue for an atmospheric summer festival of chamber music. Close by is the Église de la Conception, built for the White Penitents in 1685. Restored in the 1980s, it has a wonderfully exuberant – or over-the-top, depending on taste – baroque interior. (A third religious site, for the Black Penitents – the Chapelle des Pénitents-Noirs – stands a short distance away at the bottom of rue de Bréa.) The best way to see the square is at night, during the famous summer chamber music festival.

Salle des Mariages
Cocteau's swirling, extravagant murals succeed admirably in his aim to 'create a theatrical setting ... to offset the officialdom of a civil ceremony'.
Hôtel de Ville, place Ardoino, rue de la République. Tel: 93.57.87.87. Open: Monday to Friday, 8.30am–12.30pm, 1.30–5pm. Admission charge.

LITERARY PROVENCE

The literary tradition in Provence reaches all the way back to the troubadours, whose poems of courtly love encapsulate the most romantic aspect of medievalism. They were written in the Provençal language, which enjoyed a revival in the past century under the influence of poet Frédéric Mistral, who was awarded the Nobel Prize for Literature in 1904.

Frédéric Mistral (above); scene from *Manon des Sources* (below)

Marcel Pagnol (1895–1974) from Aubagne was a writer of novels, poems and short stories. His vision of Provence was captured in the atmospheric stories that became the award-winning films *Jean de Florette* and *Manon des Sources*, starring Gérard Depardieu and Yves Montand. Jean Giono (1895–1970) was similarly inspired by the landscapes and the people of Provence – in his case, the area around his birthplace, Manosque.

THE PERFECT WORKPLACE

Provence has arguably cast an even deeper spell over outsiders beguiled by its promise of sunshine and sensuality. In comparison to the bucolic works of its resident writers, literature of another kind was being written on the Riviera by leading American writers like F Scott

Maugham (below), Huxley (bottom) and Hemingway

Fitzgerald and Ernest Hemingway after World War I. In an era of prohibition and puritanism, they fled from what they regarded as the cultural wasteland of America to enjoy an easier lifestyle in the sun. Fitzgerald gave an evocative portrait of life in Cap d'Antibes in the 1920s in *Tender Is the Night*, but the idyll was bruised by his wife Zelda's affair with a young French aviator.

A WRITERS' COLONY

Hemingway and his wife Hadley lived in a threesome on the Riviera with the American heiress Pauline Pfeiffer before moving on. In 1930 Aldous Huxley joined a writers' colony in the South of France, his neighbours including Thomas Mann and Cyril Connolly. The English novelist Somerset Maugham bought a house in Cap Ferrat in 1926 and spent at least six months every year there until his death in 1965, entertaining such celebrities as the Aga Khan, Winston Churchill, Noël Coward and Jean Cocteau.

An earlier arrival on the Riviera was the New Zealand-born British writer Katherine Mansfield, who died tragically young from TB. On a happier note, the 18-year-old Françoise Sagan achieved fame in the 1950s with her novel *Bonjour Tristesse*, a sharply defined love story set in a villa near Cannes. Other writers closely linked with the Riviera include Graham Greene and Anthony Burgess.

Monaco

*E*ven for those used to the tightly packed, over-hyped Riviera, Monaco comes as something of a shock to the system. Not one square millimetre of Monaco is wasted. High-rise buildings are stacked up within touching distance of each other, making the most of the limited space available in this 3km-long tax haven.

Money is Monaco's *raison d'être*. The opulent main casino is the most overt manifestation of the serious wealth that underpins this home of millionaires who, perfectly legally, avoid paying any income tax. And their wealth is protected in more ways than one. Monaco has more policemen per square kilometre than anywhere else in the world. You might think that Monaco's artificiality, over-indulgence and self-satisfaction make for a pretty rich diet – and you would be correct. But you should at least sample a little of it. There are compensations: the

principality's immaculate, litter-free streets, its beautifully manicured gardens, and the undeniable spectacle of one of the world's most glamorous harbours full of some of the world's most expensive ocean-going palaces.

The densely populated principality is divided into a number of districts. Most visitor interest is concentrated in Monaco-Ville, the promontory west of the harbour (which contains the majority of the historic sites) and glitzy Monte Carlo (the casino, conference and hotel district) to the east.

MONACO

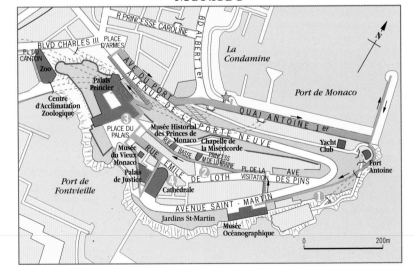

Centre d'Acclimatation Zoologique (Zoological Gardens)

Tropical flora and fauna flourish in these gardens.

Place du Canton. Tel: 93.25.18 31. Open: daily, June to September, 9am–noon, 2–7pm; March to May, 10am–noon, 2–6pm; October to February, 10am–noon, 2–5pm. Admission charge.

Jardin Exotique

Thousands of different exotic plants – including giant cacti – grow amongst rocks in this beautiful garden. You can also visit a cave with spectacular stalagmite and stalactite formations, and a museum of prehistory.

Boulevard du Jardin Exotique. Tel: 93.30.33.65. Open: daily, May to August, 9am–7pm (until 6.30pm April and September, 6pm February, March and October, 5.30pm January and November, 5pm December). Admission charge.

Musée Historial des Princes de Monaco (Wax Museum)

Episodes from the history of the Grimaldis are depicted here.

27 rue Basse. Tel: 93.30.39.05. Open: daily, February to October, 9.30am–7pm; November to January, 10.30am–5pm. Admission charge.

Musée Océanographique

Housed in a stunning neo-classical building poised over the cliff face, this museum of marine sciences contains the usual maritime specimens plus a famous 90-tank aquarium.

Avenue St-Martin. Tel: 93.15.36.00. Open: daily, June to August, 9am–8pm; April, May and September, 9am–7pm; March and October, 9am–7pm; November to February, 10am–6pm. Admission charge.

All the best boats moor in the high-society harbour in Monaco

Musée du Vieux Monaco

Paintings, pottery, old photographs, costumes and other artefacts tell the story of the Old Town.

Rue Émile de Loth. Tel: 93.50.57.28. Open: spring, summer and winter school holidays, Monday, Wednesday and Friday, 2.30–5.30pm; otherwise Wednesday 2.30–5.30pm. Free.

Palais Princier (Prince's Palace)

Outstanding features include the Italian-style gallery, the blue-and-gold Louis XV Salon, and the Throne Room. The palace's South Wing contains a museum of Napoleonic souvenirs and historic archives (same telephone number, but opening times differ from the palace).

Place du Palais. Tel: 93.25.18.31. Open: daily, June to September, 9.30am–6.30pm; October 10am–5pm. Closed: November to May. Admission charge.

Nice

*T*his noisy, seductive, teeming, vibrant city-by-the-sea takes some getting used to. You do not come to Nice for a quiet time; neither do you come for a standard seaside holiday. You come because of Nice's exhaustive stock of first-class museums; you come to sample its bubbling nightlife; you come to take a stroll down the famous promenade des Anglais; you come for business, not pleasure, for Nice is the nucleus of a dynamic southern economy dubbed the 'California of Europe'. You might – if you have the time – even spend an hour or so on the beach.

The only way to begin to get to know Nice is on foot. Many places of interest are within reasonable walking distance of the strip of coast that runs for a kilometre or so from Le Château hill along the promenade des Anglais.

The English, French and Italians have all had a hand in creating the Nice of today. English aristocrats gave the benevolent climate their stamp of approval. Italian nobility ruled here until 1860, when they handed the city over to the French and *Nizza* became Nice. This mixed bag of influences is most apparent in the central area, where you will find the convincingly Italianate

place Masséna (which really should be across the border!), the medieval Vieille Ville, the *belle époque* architecture, the extravagantly spacious gardens, the animated daily market along cours Saleya, and the main shopping streets. The one viewpoint from which it all starts to make sense is the 92m-high Le Château, not a castle but a wooded park.

Other places to visit, in addition to those listed below, include the Musée d'Art Naïf Anatole Jakovsky, Musée Franciscain et Monastère de Cimiez, Musée d'Histoire Naturelle, Musée Naval, Musée Renoir, Palais Lascaris and Villa Arson.

Musée d'Archéologie
Exhibits span the Bronze Age down to the Middle Ages. It stands on the edge of excavated 3rd-century Roman baths with 5th-century religious buildings. *Avenue Monte-Croce, Cimiez. Tel: 93.81.59.57. Open: May to September, 10am–noon, 2–6pm; October to April, 10am–noon, 2–5pm. Closed: Sunday morning, Monday and through November. Free (admission charge to excavations)*

This street in busy Nice, with its stuccoed buildings, has a distinctly Italianate air

Exhibit in the Museum of Modern Art, just one of Nice's many fine museums

Musée d'Art Moderne et d'Art Contemporain

The permanent collection consists mainly of Neo-Realism and Pop Art.
Promenade des Arts. Tel: 93.62.61.62.
Open: Wednesday to Monday, 11am–6pm (until 10pm Friday). Free.

Musée des Beaux-Arts (Museum of Fine Arts)

The gallery has a large collection of 17th- to 19th-century paintings plus sculptures.
33 avenue des Baumettes. Tel: 93.44.50.72. Open: Tuesday to Sunday, May to September, 10am–noon, 3–6pm; October to April, 10am–noon, 2–5pm. Free.

Musée Masséna

This wide-ranging historical museum has everything from sumptuous furniture to traditional costumes, art to armour.
Palais Masséna, rue de France and 35 promenade des Anglais. Tel: 93.88.11.34 or 93.88.06.22. Open: Tuesday to Sunday,
May to September, 10am–noon, 3–6pm; October to April, 10am–noon, 2–5pm. Closed: November. Free.

Musée Matisse

Matisse settled in Nice in 1917 and died here in 1954. His personal collection is displayed in a splendid 17th-century villa in Cimiez, Nice's upmarket suburb.
164 avenue des Arènes de Cimiez. Tel: 93.81.08.08. Open: Wednesday to Monday, April to September, 11am–7pm; October to March, 10am–5pm. Free.

Musée National Marc Chagall

Chagall's fabulist style is given full expression in a series of paintings, a 'Biblical Message' based on the Old Testament.
Avenue du Docteur-Ménard. Tel: 93.81.75.75. Open: Wednesday to Monday, July to September, 10am–7pm; October to June, 10am–12.30pm, 2–5.30pm. Admission charge.

ST-PAUL-DE-VENCE

Some perched villages are famous for their restaurants, others for their real estate. St-Paul is famous for its art. Galleries are everywhere, though the usual crafts and clothes shops aren't exactly thin on the ground. The village has made a lot of concessions to tourists: few of the medieval houses along its main street seem to serve their original purpose, having been converted into expensive galleries and not-so-exclusive T-shirt and fast-food joints. Nevertheless, St-Paul has charm. Its arty associations reach their zenith at the Fondation Maeght. The village even displays its cultural pretensions on its pavements, which are decorated with pebbles arranged in artistic swirls and patterns.

The main gate into the village is alongside the Café de la Place, a lovely old-fashioned café complete with *boules* pitch outside. St-Paul's unbroken ring of 16th-century walls protects a medieval village dominated by a hilltop church. The 12th-century Église de St-Paul-de-Vence has a tall 18th-century bell tower that is almost matched in height by the giant palm tree growing beside it.

The Fondation Maeght, St-Paul-de-Vence's airy and informal modern art gallery

Fondation Maeght

Created in the 1950s by collectors Aimé and Marguerite Maeght, this unique purpose-built arts centre eschews the established concepts of entrance, exit and the *sense de la visite*. Nothing is arranged conventionally. Outside, you will encounter modern sculpture set tongue-in-cheek against water, trees and stone walls. Permanent and temporary exhibitions are held in the centre's airy split-level galleries.
Route Passe-Prest. Tel. 93.32.81.63. Open: daily, July to September, 10am–7pm; October to June, 10am–12.30pm, 2.30–6pm. Admission charge.

Musée d'Histoire Locale

The most important events in the lives of the people of St-Paul are reflected in the museum's tableaux and exhibits.
Place de la Castre. Tel. 93.32.53.09. Open: Tuesday to Sunday, 10am–6pm, Monday 10.30am–5.30pm. Admission charge.

St-Paul-de-Vence is in the hills between Nice and Antibes.

SAORGE

High in the Alpes-Maritimes close to the Italian border, this village is accessible by the N204 through the Gorges de Saorge, a dramatic defile carved by the tumbling River Roya. The fortified village was built to control communications into the high country of the Haute Roya, a hybrid area of Italian and French influences which only became French territory in 1947.

Saorge, its terraces piled haphazardly one above the other on a savage slope, is a spectacular sight. This *village empilé* (stacked village) is the mountain equivalent of the perched villages along the coast. Its impossibly steep cobbled alleyways and confusing tiers of streets eventually lead up to the 15th-century Église St-Sauveur and a Franciscan monastery. Further up still is the isolated 11th-century Romanesque chapel of Madone del Poggio.

Higher up the valley, close to the border, is the unequivocally Italianate village of Tende, while to the south lies restful Breil-sur-Roya, centre of the local olive oil industry (see pages 162–3). *Saorge is close to the Italian border 47km north of Menton.*

TOURETTES-SUR-LOUP

This picturesque village is partly misnamed. Its medieval towers (*tours*) are evident enough, but the River Loup is elsewhere, in the rolling, wooded hills to the south. The village's Grand-Rue is also misleadingly named: narrow, crooked and atmospheric, it winds its way past ancient, rough-stoned houses, some of which have been converted into potteries, craft workshops and galleries, while others still await restoration.

From Tourettes, take the D2210 to Pont-du-Loup, turning northwards along the D6 for the craggy Gorges du Loup. The narrow road, chiselled out of the rock face, wriggles up a steep-sided valley beside the foaming river. At the top end of the gorge, return south on the D3, which climbs to give wonderful views down into the vertical-sided valley. *Tourettes-sur-Loup is about 22km northeast of Grasse.*

Saorge, a 'stacked village' dramatically perched on the mountain side

ART IN PROVENCE

The vivid colours and intense light of the South of France have enticed many artists to Provence, including Van Gogh (see pages 56–7), Monet and Renoir in the 19th century, and Matisse and Picasso in the 20th.

19TH CENTURY

Claude Monet first visited the region in 1883 and returned in 1888 to stay in Antibes and Juan-les-Pins. He followed the custom of the age by spending winter and early spring in the south and shrewdly painted local beauty spots to attract collectors.

Auguste Renoir spent the winter of 1889–90 in the south and settled in

Cagnes-sur-Mer in 1905. Crippled by rheumatoid arthritis, he continued to paint with a brush wedged between his rigid fingers, completing more than

Facing page: Provence as seen
by Cézanne (top) and Monet

Renoir (right) and
Chagall both settled
on the Riviera

6,000 pictures in his lifetime.

Paul Cézanne was a home-grown talent. He spent much of his life in his birthplace, Aix-en-Provence (where he died in 1906), gradually establishing a reputation which today places him as a master of Post-Impressionism and one of the forerunners of modern art.

equal, moving to St-Jean-Cap-Ferrat in 1949. In the 1950s Nice produced the school of artists known as Nouveaux Realistes, who reacted against the Abstract Expressionism popular in America and the lyrical Abstraction of Paris. One of its exponents, Yves Klein, coated the bodies of nude models with paint and ordered them to crawl over the canvases. Whatever would Van Gogh have made of that?

Modern master, Picasso

20TH CENTURY

Henri Matisse and Raoul Dufy were among the *fauves* ('wild beasts'), so called because of their aggressive use of strong colour, who also followed the Impressionists. The most influential artist of the 20th century, Pablo Picasso, often spent his summers at Juan-les-Pins between the wars, and in 1946 he left Paris for good to settle in the Riviera. The lifestyle had a liberating effect, and even in extreme old age he created 1,000 works of art in five years. A lifetime of creativity ended in April 1973, when he died at the age of 92.

The success of Picasso and Matisse offended another great artist associated with the Riviera, Marc Chagall. He settled there to show the world he was their

VALLAURIS

If you do not like pottery, then give Vallauris a miss. The town's love affair with pots is flaunted quite unselfconsciously. Oversized urns, serving as giant flowerpots, line the smart shopping streets in the modern town beneath the old quarter of the Vieille Ville with its Renaissance château.

Vallauris's pottery pedigree dates back to Roman times. By the end of World War II, the industry was on its last legs. Revival came when Pablo Picasso took an interest, spending two prolific years at the Madoura pottery workshop in the town. Other artists, including Chagall, followed in his wake. Vallauris was back in the pottery business.

Most of the potteries – of varying quality and value – are located along the main street, avenue Georges-Clémenceau; the Madoura pottery, which still sells Picasso designs, is off the main street along avenue des Anciens Combattants d'AFN. In the place de la Libération, the town's main square and marketplace, is the life-size bronze statue *Man Holding a Sheep*, Picasso's gift to the town in 1950.

Vallauris is famous for its pottery

Musée Municipal

Housed in the château, the museum contains an excellent collection of ceramics – including pieces by Picasso – and paintings by Italian artist Alberto Magnelli (1888–1971).
Place de la Libération. Tel: 93.64.16.05 or 93.64.18.05. Open: Wednesday to Monday 10am–noon, 2–5pm. Admission charge.

Musée National Picasso

In 1952 Picasso decorated the walls of Vallauris's 13th-century Romanesque chapel (in the château's courtyard) with a huge *War and Peace* tableau.
Place de la Libération. Tel: 93.64.16.05 or 93.64.18.05. Open: Wednesday to Monday, April to September, 10am–noon, 2–5pm; October to March, 2–6pm. Admission charge.

Musée de la Poterie

Pottery demonstrations take place in this faithful reconstruction of a turn-of-the-century workshop.
Rue Sicard. Tel: 93.64.66.51. Open: daily 9am–7pm. Admission charge.

Vallauris is in the hills between Cannes and Antibes.

VENCE

After its high-flying neighbour, St-Paul-de-Vence (see page 112), Vence brings you back down to earth. There is nothing particularly arty about Vence, a town that is too busy serving its resident population of 14,000. The thousands who have moved here in recent decades, attracted by the gentle climate and the booming sun-belt industries, have created something of an urban sprawl around the old town. But they have also

Shaded cafés in the old town of Vence provide a pleasant lunch-stop

brought a vitality and renewed purpose to Vence, without damaging the inherent charm of its historic centre.

A ring of medieval ramparts and gateways protected Vieux Vence (Old Vence). Much of the defence remains, most notably at the Porte du Peyra, a 15th-century fortified gate with 17th-century additions. Place du Peyra and place Clemenceau are charming tree-shaded open areas. The latter gives access to the former cathedral, dating from the 10th century but incorporating Roman fragments and later additions. The latest of all, in the baptistery, is the most striking: a mosaic by Marc Chagall depicting Moses in the bulrushes.

The town has strong links with many painters and writers. In the 1920s it became an artistic haven, attracting the likes of Gide, Dufy and D H Lawrence, who died here in 1930 of tuberculosis contracted in England.

Chapelle du Rosaire

Henri Matisse designed and decorated this chapel between 1947 and 1951. The stark use of colour in his bold black-and-white ceramic murals – a surprise to many – finds a counterpoint in his marvellous stained-glass windows. *466 avenue Henri-Matisse. Tel: 93.58.03.26 or 93.58.06.38 (Office de Tourisme). Open: Tuesday and Thursday, 10–11.30am, 2.30–5.30pm. Other times by prior arrangement. Closed: November to mid-December. Free.*

Colourful church façade in Vence

Monaco

This walk concentrates on Monaco-Ville, the rocky promontory above the harbour dominated by the Palais Princier (Prince's Palace). In comparison to the hustle and bustle of the port below and the shops and casinos of Monte Carlo to the east, this part of the principality – the picturesque Old Town, a mixture of narrow streets, open spaces and gardens – seems positively sedate. For details of the main sites listed, please see pages 108–9. *The walk can be comfortably completed in half a day.*

From La Racasse hairpin (a name familiar to fans of Formula One Grand Prix racing) in the La Condamine harbour and business district, walk along quai Antoine 1er, taking a short detour left along the sea wall to the mouth of the port. Return to the yacht club on the quay, then climb the steps up towards the tubby-looking Fort Antoine, continuing the climb into the gardens (signposted Palais, Musée).

1 QUAY WALK AND GARDENS

The quay walk and gardens give you some idea of what Monaco must have been like before the developers took over. The quieter side of the harbour leads to restful, shady gardens rising above Fort Antoine, an 18th-century defensive fortification now used as an outdoor theatre (tel: 93.15.80.00). *Walk through the gardens to the Musée Océanographique, then take the pedestrianised street opposite – ruelle des Écoles – for place de la Visitation, turning left here for rue Princess Marie de Lorraine.*

2 RUE PRINCESS MARIE DE LORRAINE

This cobbled street leads to the heart of the Old Town. The Chapelle de la

Monaco's cathedral contains the tomb of the much-loved Princess Grace

du Palais is a natural vantage point. Lined with cannons cast under Louis XIV, it looks down directly into the harbour, across to high-rise Monte Carlo and along the coast as far east as the Cape of Bordighera in Italy.

Leave place du Palais by rue Colonel Bellando de Castro, which brings you to the Palais de Justice and cathedral.

The royal palace of Monaco (above), and changing the guard (right)

Miséricorde, built 1639–45, was the seat of the Brotherhood of the Black Penitents, and contains a remarkable figure of Christ carved in wood.

Continue down rue Basse, a very narrow street lined with shops and cafés, to the Musée Historial des Princes de Monaco (Wax Museum). From here, the street becomes even narrower before opening out into the huge open square, place du Palais.

3 PLACE DU PALAIS

Place du Palais fronts the Palais Princier, the home of the Monégasque royal family, a mainly 19th-century building castellated for decorative effect only. The Changing of the Guard takes place here at 11.55am every day, a ceremony performed in full dress uniform (white in summer, black in winter). The lofty place

4 CATHÉDRALE

The 19th-century cathedral, built in Romanesque-Byzantine style on the site of a 13th-century church dedicated to St Nicholas, contains tombs of former princes of Monaco. An episcopal throne in white marble and early 16th-century reredos are amongst its noteworthy features, though the cathedral's most-visited shrine is the tomb of Princess Grace.

Follow rue de l'Église between the Palais de Justice and the cathedral, turning left along rue Émile de Loth for the Musée du Vieux Monaco (Museum of Old Monaco). Return to place du Palais and descend this rocky outcrop by La Rampe Major, a staircase in the side of the cliff. Cross avenue de la Porte Neuve and follow avenue du Port back to the harbourside.

Alpes-de-Haute-Provence

*P*rovence's away-from-it-all *département* – and its least populated – is the meeting ground between Mediterranean and Alpine influences. Pastoral foothills in the south eventually rise into rocky mountain ranges, snow-capped for much of the year. Apart from developments along the Durance Valley, the Alpes-de-Haute-Provence is largely unaffected by change. Its rugged character and robust, grey-stoned mountain villages make it the least Provençal of the region's five *départements*.

CASTELLANE

Castellane's location at the eastern approach of the Grand Cañon du Verdon (see pages 130–1) guarantees a healthy number of summer visitors. Its market square, place Marcel-Sauvaire, is

Castellane, dominated by a massive chapel-crowned limestone rock

set against a backdrop of steep hills. The steepest of all is the huge rocky outcrop, looming menacingly over the town, which is topped by the little pilgrimage chapel of Notre-Dame-du-Roc. The 18th-century chapel is a 30-minute walk along a path that passes the Tour Pentagonale, a five-sided fortified tower that was part of the town's medieval defences.

Castellane is an excellent centre for outdoor pursuits in and around the Grand Cañon, with equipment shops and agencies covering the whole sporting spectrum, from mountain biking to white-water rafting.
Castellane is 63km northwest of Grasse.

DIGNE-LES-BAINS

Digne's famous spa is hidden in a secluded, wooded valley a few kilometres from the centre. Whilst the *thermes* have an ongoing air of prosperity, the town itself shows a few signs of neglect. The cathedral, a grim-looking hulk enlivened by a tall campanile, needs some care and attention. The open spaces of place Général-de-Gaulle are much more visitor-friendly, though lacking the animated atmosphere of other French towns. But do not be discouraged by

ALPES-DE-HAUTE-PROVENCE

these negatives. Digne, which enjoys a beautiful, mountain-ringed location, is a restrained place with an understated charm typical of many spa towns.

Musée de Digne

Archaeology, art and natural history are all covered here.
64 boulevard Gassendi. Tel: 92.31.45.29. Open: Tuesday to Sunday 10am–noon, 2–6pm (until 5pm on Sunday). Admission charge.

Résidence Alexandra David-Néel

The house of the fiercely individualistic Alexandra David-Néel recalls her fascination with all things Tibetan.
28 avenue du Maréchal-Juin. Tel: 92.31.32.38. Open: daily, July to September, 10.30am–5pm (4 guided tours); October to June, 10.30am–4pm (3 guided tours). Admission charge.

Digne-les-Bains is 117km northwest of Grasse.

ENTREVAUX

The town makes no secret of its strategic importance. You enter by crossing the fairytale Porte Royale, a remarkable fortified bridge over the River Var. But that is just the beginning, for the citadel that fulfils the serious defensive role is perched high on a rock above the rooftops, an eyrie from which it keeps a threatening, all-seeing eye on the valley.

The original fortification was strengthened in the late 17th century by Vauban, Louix XIV's military architect, to defend this frontier town in France's disputes with Savoy. The only way up is along a zigzagging pathway cut into the rock. If you can't face the climb, then content yourself with Entrevaux's 17th-century cathedral which is built into the town's street-level defences. As a respite from Entrevaux's overpoweringly medieval air, you can retreat into the decidedly 20th-century little museum that celebrates the motor car.

Citadel open: daily, July–August, 9am–noon, 3–6pm; March–June and September–October, 10am–noon, 3–5pm. Closed: November to February. Further details from the Office de Tourisme, tel: 93.05.46.73 (summer); also the Town Hall, tel: 93.05.40.04.
Entrevaux is on the N202, 72km northwest of Nice.

FORCALQUIER

This unexpectedly engaging small town lies at the heart of Provence between the Mediterranean and the Alps, a hilly, sunny area in which olive and beech trees grow side by side. Forcalquier has all the trappings of a long history – a ruined hilltop citadel, cathedral, wealth of other religious sites, Romanesque monuments, weathered Renaissance façades – but little of the fame enjoyed by other heritage-rich towns.

The town's Golden Age was in early medieval times when the counts of Forcalquier created an independent state, which lasted for over a century. Unlike places such as Aix, in which every

The medieval fortified town of Entrevaux commands the River Var

ancient feature is assiduously cherished, Forcalquier is not meticulous about preserving its past.

If you prefer your historic sites in their original state, then this is the place for you. Dominating place du Bourguet, the central square, is the former Cathédrale Notre-Dame, a large complex pile dating from the early 12th century and in dire need of restoration. Opposite is the Couvent de la Visitation, an old convent and chapel of delicately carved stonework that have unceremoniously been converted into a town hall, museum – and cinema!

The old town lies behind the cathedral, an area of 13th- to 18th-century houses that look their age. Place St-Michel's 16th-century fountain has an explicit carving demonstrating that medieval sexual practices in France deserve a mention in the *Kama Sutra*.

A short distance south of Forcalquier are two interesting places to visit – the Château de Sauvan and the Observatoire de Haute-Provence.

Château de Sauvan

This opulent 18th-century château, set in splendid grounds, looks like a refugee from the Loire Valley.
About 7km south of Forcalquier on the N100. Tel: 92.75.05.64. Open: July to September, daily (except Saturday) for guided tour only at 3.30pm; October to June, Sunday for guided tour only at 3.30pm. Admission charge.

Couvent des Cordeliers

Forcalquier's 13th-century Franciscan monastery preserves its scriptorium, library, monastic hall and terraces.
Boulevard des Martyrs de la Résistance. Tel: 92.75.02.38, or 92.75.10.02 (Office de Tourisme). Open: July to mid-

Forcalquier's church of Notre Dame de Provence was once a cathedral

September, daily 11am–5.30pm (5 guided tours); May to June, mid-September to October, Sunday 2.30–4.30pm (3 guided tours). Admission charge.

Musée de Forcalquier

The museum has displays of local archaeology, history and ethnography.
Place du Bourguet. Tel: 92.75.10.02 (Office de Tourisme). Open: daily, July to September, 10am–noon, 3–7pm; otherwise 2–4pm. Admission charge.

Observatoire de Haute-Provence

The National Centre for Scientific Research sited its observatory here because of the area's clear skies and lack of industrial pollution.
Accessible via St-Michel l'Observatoire off the N100 southwest of Forcalquier. For details of visiting times, ask at Forcalquier's Office de Tourisme, tel: 92.75.10.02.

Forcalquier is 83km northeast of Aix-en-Provence.

Walk under the arch of the Porte Saunerie to enter the old town of Manosque

pedestrianised rue-Grande is a plaque announcing the birthplace, on 30 March 1895, of writer Jean Giono (1895–1970), who wrote about the people and places of this part of Provence. (The Centre Jean Giono, at 1 boulevard Elémir-Bourges, looks at the writer's life and work; open: 9am–noon and 2–6pm (except Sunday, and Monday morning); tel: 92.72.76.10. See also 'Literary Provence', pages 106–7.) A little further along rue-Grande is the Église St-Sauveur with a handsome, plain façade and ornate wrought-iron campanile (a bell cage, built to withstand the mistral wind, which you see on churches and monuments all across Provence).

This is a town that rewards aimless wandering. You will come across many pleasing details: the shady fountains, the

Le froid ('Cold') statue in Manosque

GRAND CAÑON DU VERDON

See pages 130–1.

MANOSQUE

This bustling town is set on a hillside above the wide Durance Valley. Not so long ago, only 5,000 people lived here, a figure that has now quadrupled. A strategic location, good communications by autoroute, a nearby nuclear research centre and an enviable climate have turned Manosque into the archetypal Provençal boom town. The tell-tale signs of affluence are everywhere: in the neatly refurbished streets of the old town, the solidly middle-income shops and the well-dressed populace.

Manosque's focus of interest lies within the relatively small area of the old town, defined by a circular one-way traffic system. You can enter on foot through Porte Saunerie, a tall, fortified gateway that looks like a disembodied castle tower. A short distance along the

SANTONS

Folk art and religious faith come together in Provence in the Nativity scenes that occupy proud places in the home at Christmas time. The figures, known as _santons_ (little saints), are made of baked clay formed from plaster-cast moulds. They are painted in meticulous detail with acrylics and range from thimble-size to doll-size.

A town in miniature

These crèches are unique, for they contain not only the Biblical figures of Jesus, Mary, Joseph, shepherds and Wise Men, but also a supporting cast representing people in a 19th-century Provençal town. Wearing clothes of that period, the _santons_ depict a cross-section of society: farmers, fishermen, shopkeepers, teachers, businessmen, priests and so on. There are sometimes more than a hundred figures on display, as well as intricately fashioned models of stone houses surrounding the stable. Twigs of rosemary and thyme depict trees, while hillsides are made out of pebbles and moss.

Spreading custom

The custom began in Marseille early in the 19th century, when the original _santonniers_ (_santon_ makers) modelled their figurines on the village characters portrayed in the Nativity plays known as _pastorales_ and the ingenious _crèches parlantes_ ('talking crèches' with speaking marionettes). The custom spread to neighbouring towns and villages and has since become a popular Provençal tradition. Marseille and the nearby city of Aix-en-Provence are still the _santon_-making centres of Provence, and a great _santon_ fair is held in Marseille for two weeks each winter. Although especially linked to the festive season, _santons_ can be bought at craft shops and fairs in Provence at any time of the year.

Colourful _santons_ in 19th-century dress, sold as souvenirs nowadays

decorative touches in the mellow stonework, the beautifully carved doorways (look out especially for the Renaissance carvings on the portal of Manosque's other church, the Église Notre-Dame-de-Romigier).
Manosque is 50km northeast of Aix-en-Provence.

WILDLIFE

The abundance of plant and animal life in Provence makes it a fascinating destination for naturalists. Wild rosemary and thyme grow on the pine-scented hillsides, while pyramidal cypress trees bring a darker, more dramatic accent of green to the surroundings. Vines flourish on sunny, stony slopes and plains, sometimes sharing a valley floor or hillside with olive groves.

Another distinct feature of Provence is the *garrigue* or *maquis*, names given to the dense undergrowth of stunted, hard-leafed evergreens, shrubs and bushes that harbour a wealth of animals. Orchids thrive in some areas, and edible fungi include truffles, which are gathered in Vaucluse with the aid of trained dogs. Palms and cacti add to the variety the region holds for visitors from cooler climes.

The famously expensive black truffles of Provence

The flowers of Provence attract butterflies of many species, and moths are to be found in profusion. Summer visitors among the bird population include the gaudy bee-eater, which feeds off insects it catches on the wing. The Camargue is a world-class nature reserve renowned for its exceptional birdlife, which includes pink flamingos, marsh- and seabirds, waterfowl and birds of prey. Look out for egrets, perched on the back of cattle, feeding off the Camargue's itchy insect life.

Wild boars find shelter in the protective *garrigue*. Together with quails, pheasants, partridges – and practically anything else with four legs or a pair of wings – they attract the attention of the hunting-mad Provençals outside the protected areas. Other Provençal residents include beavers, many reptiles (tortoises, snakes, lizards, etc) and even a few golden eagles in the remoter mountains.

You will not have to look too hard to

Just some of the
abundant wildlife
of the region

find the cicada with its insistent
click, a creature synonymous
with a hot Provençal summer.
And do not be too concerned if
you see a scorpion scurrying out
from under a rock – the French
variety will, at worst, give you
something like a wasp sting.

Spectacularly situated Moustiers has produced fine ceramics for centuries

Its location is breathtaking. The village is built into the side of a V-shaped ravine split by a rushing watercourse, a fairy-tale setting. Here you will find pottery shops ... and pottery shops ... and pottery shops. Moustiers pottery has been famous for centuries. After a spell in the doldrums, the industry revived in the 1930s and now makes a thriving living off its glazed decorative ware.

Another reason for the village's popularity is its location at the western gateway to the Grand Cañon du Verdon (see pages 130–1). In summer, congestion is a problem. The sensible advice is to come early or late in the day – or, better still, in the spring or autumn.

Exploration is a delight when you have the place to yourself. The pretty cobbled square above the church leads to a steep pathway that climbs high up the side of the ravine to a second religious site, the 12th-century Chapelle Notre-Dame-de-Beauvoir. Higher still, suspended on a 227m-long chain, is a famous curiosity – a man-sized star, supposedly placed there by a knight returning from the Crusades (the existing version, it should be pointed out, is 1957-vintage).

Musée de la Faïence (Pottery Museum)

Exhibits trace the history of Moustiers pottery.
Place du Presbytère. Tel: 92.74.67.84 (Office de Tourisme). Open: Wednesday to Monday, April to October, 9am–noon, 2–6pm. Admission charge.

Moustiers-Ste-Marie is 48km south of Digne-les-Bains.

MOUSTIERS-STE-MARIE

Moustiers is invariably criticised for being a tourist trap. This is unfair. The criticisms, one suspects, are based on pure aesthetics: whereas some places along the coast are a lost cause, Moustiers could be even more attractive without the souvenir and gift shops.

RIEZ

Neighbouring Moustiers-Ste-Marie grabs all the attention, leaving Riez to its fate as an obscure country town. The visitors who do come – accidentally or otherwise – will discover a great deal of antiquity, presented without any of the usual fuss or flourish. Riez was an important meeting of the ways for the Romans. Four Roman columns, the remnants of a temple, stand like a piece of surreal art in a field on the outskirts of town. The original Roman settlement was on the hill of Mont St-Maxime above, the site of a 17th-century chapel and a good viewpoint across the surrounding lavender fields.

Further echoes of Riez's former – and now faded – glory can be traced amongst the rich Renaissance façades along Grand-Rue, the early Christian baptistery next to the excavated site of the cathedral, and the grandly proportioned Hôtel de Ville (Town Hall), originally an episcopal palace.
Riez is 42km south of Digne-les-Bains.

SISTERON

You need not be a military historian to understand Sisteron's strategic value. It grew up at a point where the Durance Valley funnels into a narrow defile between two enormous outcrops. Surmounting the western rock is an awesome, grey-stone citadel, guardian of a crucial gateway into Provence from the Alps.

The medieval citadel stands on a site that has been fortified for thousands of years. From the summit, high above the single bridge across the river, the citadel's grey mass is mirrored by the

outcrop of Rocher de la Baume opposite. Below, tall dwellings line a maze of narrow streets known locally as *andrônes*. Instead of having the usual stone facing, they are rendered as protection against the cold draught from the Alps, giving Sisteron a robust mountain character rather than a sybaritic Mediterranean warmth.

Citadelle

Before it suffered Allied bombing in 1944, this towering fortress-cum-prison was even more impressive.
Tel: 92.61.27.57. Open: daily, March to November, 8.30am–7pm. Admission charge.

Sisteron is 48km south of Gap.

The immense Rocher de la Baume, opposite Sisteron on the River Durance

Grand Cañon du Verdon

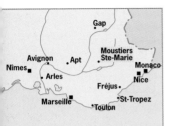

Some much-touted natural spectacles prove to be an anti-climax. The Grand Cañon du Verdon is categorically not amongst them. This first-division site is, in places, literally breathtaking. A giant slash cut deep into the earth's crust with heart-stopping 800m-drops and awesome vistas, this is one of the not-to-be-missed places on any visit to Provence. A road runs right around the cañon on both sides, thus allowing a convenient circular car tour of the entire spectacle. That is the good news. The bad news is its popularity. In summer, this route is a busy one. You will have to keep a wary eye not only on the road, which skirts some truly fearsome cliff edges, but also on other sightseeing motorists. Far better to come in the quieter autumn or spring, when you will have this stunning phenomenon almost all to yourself. You should also bear in mind that petrol stations in this remote corner are few and far between. *With stops, the tour will take all day.*

From Moustiers-Ste-Marie (see page 128) take the D957 south, turning left on to the D19, which winds its way up through scrub land to Aiguines.

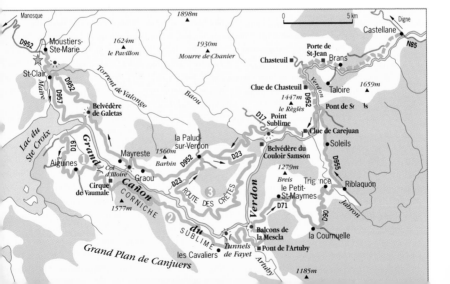

1 AIGUINES

The pretty hilltop village of Aiguines enjoys wonderful views westwards to the Lac de Ste-Croix – a huge man-made sheet of unnaturally blue water fed by the River Verdon – and the strange, flat-topped plateau above it.

From Aiguines, the serpentine road climbs up the Col d'Illoire for the first glimpse into the achingly deep canyon.

2 CORNICHE SUBLIME

The Col d'Illoire marks the start of the Corniche Sublime, which runs along the canyon's southern rim. Mossy, sheer-sided cliffs line the walls of a narrow defile carved by the Verdon, a sliver of water that runs along a sometimes rocky, sometimes placid course in the riverbed so far below. Along the corniche are noticeboards giving details of walks of different lengths and gradations into the canyon. Please note that some of these paths are very steep, so choose your trail carefully.

Beyond Les Cavaliers the road enters the Tunnels de Fayet, then crosses the River Artuby, a tributary of the Verdon. A short distance after the bridge, stop off at the Balcons de la Mescla, a viewpoint overlooking a great loop in the Verdon. This is your last glimpse of the gorge and river on the southern leg of the journey. Follow the D71 eastwards, turning left along the D90 towards Trigance, then left on the D955 for Pont de Soleils and the D952. Here, you can take a detour east to Castellane (see page 120). A few kilometres west of Pont de Soleils on the D952, take a short detour after the tunnel to the Belvédère du Couloir Samson, which ends in a deep cleft beside the rushing Verdon. Return to the D952 for the lofty viewpoint of 783m-high Point Sublime. Continue westwards, turning left along the Route des Crêtes (D23).

A dizzying look down into the mighty Grand Cañon du Verdon

3 ROUTE DES CRÊTES

By now you may be tempted to miss the D23 loop, having had a surfeit of viewpoints. But on this tour, the best is kept for last. The Route des Crêtes is a must, eclipsing even the Corniche Sublime. There are so many breathtaking *belvédères* – and hair-raising hairpin bends – that it is impossible to describe them all (the 1,285m-high Belvédère du Pas de la Baou is particularly stunning).

Rejoin the D952 at La Palud-sur-Verdon, passing the point where the river suddenly escapes from the canyon into the lake on the return to Moustiers.

ROUTE NAPOLÉON

The return by Napoléon Bonaparte from exile on Elba in March 1815 marks one of the most audacious episodes in French history. Napoléon's 'Hundred Days' took him from fugitive status in southern France back to power in Paris and on to Waterloo and his final defeat, after which he was permanently incarcerated on the island of St Helena. After escaping from the island of Elba, Napoléon landed at Golfe-Juan, marching northwards with a small

The sign of the eagle and a roadside chalet mark Napoléon's route after he fled Elba

band of followers to reclaim Paris. His route took him through Cannes, Mouans-Sartoux, St-Vallier-de-Thierry, Escragnolles and Castellane, where he crossed the Verdon by the now disused stone bridge. He was hardly greeted with open arms, and had to avoid Grasse, continuing on through the hills and mountains on stony, obscure tracks. It was not until he reached Gap that he began to regain some of his hero status.

His march through the mountains is commemorated by the winding N85, now known as the Route Napoléon, built in the 1930s.

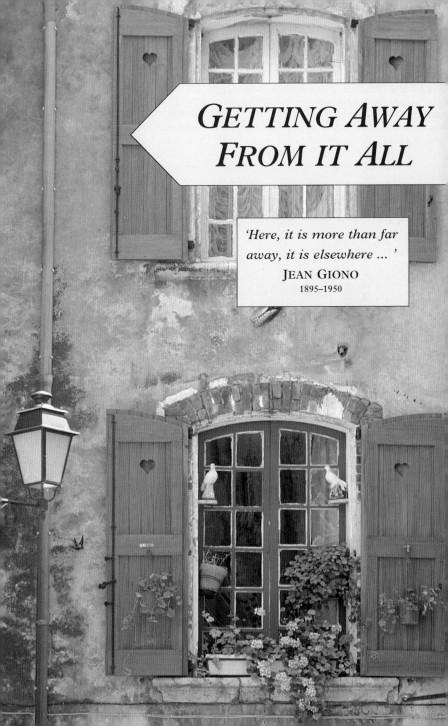

GETTING AWAY FROM IT ALL

'Here, it is more than far away, it is elsewhere ...'
JEAN GIONO
1895–1950

The cliff-top fort at Aiguèze stands above the River Ardeche

ARDÈCHE GORGES

The Gorges of the Ardèche get you away from Provence rather than away from it all. Only a short distance across the Rhône Valley from the Vaucluse, it would be pedantic in the extreme to ignore these gorges, one of the great natural wonders of France, even though they are technically outside the area. The gorges were formed by the River Ardèche, which has cut a deep channel through the limestone strata of a high plateau. They lie between Vallon-Pont-d'Arc (the main 'resort' town for the gorges) and St-Martin-d'Ardèche (a smaller tourist centre across the river from the cliff-top fort at Aiguèze). The as-the-crow-flies distance between the two is a mere 18km, which almost trebles when you follow the serpentine road that imitates the convoluted, looping progress of the river.

There are two ways of seeing the gorges. You can drive the corniche road, the D290, which has many spectacular viewpoints along the way. Access by foot into the deepest recesses of the gorge is impossible from these high *belvédères*: you will have to be content to stand and gaze. The only easy access to river level is at the beginning and end of the gorges, where there are popular swimming and sunbathing 'beach' areas.

The second method, by canoe, is far more rewarding. Canoe hire is extremely well organised from the two main centres, Vallon-Pont-d'Arc and St-Martin, with transport laid on for the outward or return leg of the journey. Make sure that you get good advice about the different sections of the river. Some parts are calm and easy, so little or no previous experience is required (though you must be able to swim!). Others, involving rapids, should only be tackled by the more experienced. You will be given tuition if necessary and full equipment (life jackets, waterproof containers, etc). Canoes can be hired for anything from half a day to two days (overnight camping is permitted). Water conditions range from calm to fast-flowing. The best time for novices is between June and August, when conditions are at their best and other canoeists are present in reassuringly high numbers. As an alternative to the do-it-yourself approach, there are trips piloted by experienced boatmen (ask at Vallon-Pont-d'Arc's Office de Tourisme for details, tel: 75.88.04.01).

The journey starts at Vallon-Pont-d'Arc. Within a few kilometres you will come across the Ardèche's most-photographed feature, the famous Pont-d'Arc, a natural arch 34m high and 59m wide (also accessible from the D290). From here, the river is shut away for

Canoes paddling under the Pont d'Arc are a familiar sight in the Gorges de l'Ardeche

30km, looping and meandering within an inaccessible chasm lined with towering walls of rock rising to 300m.

The D290 runs along the northern rim of the gorges. Its most spectacular section is the Haute Corniche (High Corniche) about two-thirds of the way along to St-Martin. Belvédère de la Madeleine, a short walk from the road, and the roadside Belvédère de la Cathédrale are tremendous viewpoints overlooking the highest part of the gorge.

AVEN D'ORGNAC

This is one of Europe's finest showcaves. *Near Barjac south of the gorges. Tel: 75.38.62.51. Open: daily, March to mid-November, 9.30am–noon, 2–6pm (until 5pm March, October and November). Admission charge.*

AVEN DE MARZAL

This attraction offers tours of an underground cave system, museum, and prehistoric 'zoo' with life-size dinosaurs. *Near St-Remèze north of the gorges. Tel: 75.04.12.45. Open: daily, mid-April to September, 9am–6pm; March to mid-April and October to November, Saturday and Sunday, 11am–6pm. Admission charge.*

CANOE HIRE

There are many operators offering more or less the same service. Here are two:

Alpha Bateaux, Pierre Peschier, route des Gorges, Vallon-Pont-d'Arc. Tel: 75.88.08.29.

Aventure Canoes, avenue Jean-Jaurès/route de Ruoms, Vallon-Pont-d'Arc. Tel: 75.37.18.14.

Simplicity and austerity characterise the Cistercian Abbaye du Thoronet

ABBAYE DU THORONET

This secluded abbey lies hidden in the Forêt de la Darboussière (Darboussière Forest) north of the A8 autoroute in the Haut-Var. Together with the Abbaye de Sénanque (see page 35) and the Abbaye de Silvacane (see page 51), it is one of the 'three Provençal sisters' founded by the Cistercians in the 12th century. The earliest – and possibly the finest – of the three, it bears all the hallmarks of the Cistercians' ascetic approach. Its austere simplicity combined with harmonious proportions gives it a rare beauty.

The most straightforward approaches are either via Brignoles in the west or Draguignan in the east. Tel: 94.73.87.13. Open: April to September, Monday to Saturday 9am–7pm; Sunday 9am–noon, 2–7pm; October to March, 9am–noon, 2–5pm. Admission charge.

MASSIF DES MAURES

If you want to escape from the crowded coast between Hyères and St-Tropez, then head inland into the densely wooded, sparsely populated hills of the Massif des Maures, the oldest mountain range in Provence. Its name derives from the Provençal *maouro*, used to describe this upland's dark cover of cork oak, chestnut and pine.

There are a few tortuous, twisting roads through the mountains, though the Maures – which rise to over 700m – are best explored on foot (the cross-country GR9 path takes in most of the high ridges). La Garde-Freinet, the tiny 'capital' of the Maures, was France's main cork-producing town in the 19th century. It still makes a living from the local cork oak, though nowadays diversifying into cork craft ornaments for the tourists. Its ruined medieval castle marks the site of an earlier stronghold occupied by the feared Saracens.

To the southwest, in the heart of the Maures, is the ancient village of Collobrières. Confectionery made from sweet chestnuts has now replaced its cork industry. A mountain pass northwards climbs to Notre-Dame-des-Anges, a pilgrimage site almost at the summit of the Maures, which enjoys predictably panoramic views.

MONTAGNE DE LURE

This mountain, a near sister to the slightly higher Mont Ventoux (see pages 48–9), rises to 1,826m above Sisteron and the Durance Valley. Not as well-served by roads (nor as heavily featured in guidebooks) as Mont Ventoux, its wooded slopes and barren summit offer a real chance of escape.

The mountain can be approached from north or south. For a north-south tour, leave Sisteron on the N85, taking

Above: sweet chestnuts for sale in the Massif des Maures; right: cork oak tree

the D946 through the pretty Jabron Valley. Then turn left on to the D53 (closed in winter), which winds along the base of a natural amphitheatre for about 5km before it starts the ascent of Lure's forested slopes.

Aire de St-Robert is an attractive picnic area, the starting point for a number of woodland walks. From here, the road surface becomes poorer for a few kilometres, though the views soon make the effort worthwhile: through the trees you will catch glimpses of the snow-capped Alps as well as the Forêt Domaniale du Jabron, which covers Lure's thickly wooded foothills.

At the 1,597m-high Col du Pas de la Graille, trees give way to patchy moorland, bare rock and even better views. If you are feeling energetic, you can park the car here and follow a footpath the final few kilometres to the summit of Signal de Lure.

The summit, like that of Ventoux, bristles with strange-looking telecommunications equipment. A dizzy 360-degree panorama seems to encompass most of southern France, from the jagged profiles of the Alps to the plateaux and plains leading down to the coast.

The descent of the mountain is on the much better engineered – and wider – D113 to sleepy St-Etienne (nervous drivers might prefer to go up as well as down on this road).

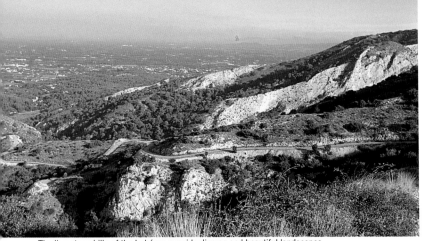

The limestone hills of the Lubéron provide diverse and beautiful landscapes

PARC NATUREL RÉGIONAL DU LUBÉRON

The Lubéron Regional Natural Park, bounded in the south by the Durance River and in the north by the beginnings of the Vaucluse Plateau, is a 60km-long chain of mountains rising to over 1,100m. The park consists of two parts: the Petit Lubéron in the west near Cavaillon, a rugged area of gorges and ravines, and the higher Grand Lubéron between Apt and Manosque in the east.

In the hierarchy of protected areas in France, a Regional Natural Park comes second to a National Park. The Lubéron was declared a Regional Park in 1977 because of the special nature of its landscapes and local traditions. Unlike a National Park, where preservation of a wilderness area is paramount, a Regional Park attempts to balance conservation with appropriate commercial activities, including tourism.

In many ways, the Lubéron takes its character from its villages, which are mostly strung out below its long spine of mountains. Human settlement, as much as natural forces, has shaped the Lubéron's beautiful landscapes. Its hilltop villages (familiar to readers of Peter Mayle's *A Year in Provence*) are surrounded by vast patches of cultivated land, its higher pastures are tended by sheep farmers, and its ochre cliffs have been mined for dye.

The Lubéron's fractured landscapes of high limestone cliffs, scrub, shrub and forest display a wonderful diversity. Sunny south-facing slopes are clothed in an aromatic Mediterranean vegetation, while oaks grow along its cooler, more humid northern escarpment. Diversity is the keynote here, for the Lubéron's rich flora and fauna include holm and downy oak, cedar, pine, cypress, rosemary, honeysuckle, lavender, eagle, owl, wild boar and beaver.

Full information on the park, including walking and cycle routes, is available at the Maison des Pays du Lubéron in Apt (see page 25). Pages 46–7 feature a car tour of the Petit Lubéron.

PARC NATIONAL DU MERCANTOUR

In terms of outright environmental protection, this National Park is one notch up on the Lubéron Regional Park (see explanation opposite). The Mercantour, roughly 90km by 30km, runs close to the French/Italian border more or less from Sospel to Barcelonnette embracing big-league mountains consistently in the 2,500–3,000m range. Most of the park lies in the Alpes-Maritimes, with a small northern section in the Alpes-de-Haute-Provence.

Exploration of this challenging wilderness should not be taken lightly. Walkers should always expect the worst: parts of the park have a long, snowy winter that can last from October to June. Even in summer nothing is predictable, for weather conditions can change alarmingly in a short space of time and from valley to valley.

The Mercantour was Italian territory until after World War II, when it was ceded to France and became a nature reserve. Its highest mountain is Mont Pelat, a 3,051m peak that rises above Lac d'Allos, a mountain lake itself at over 2,200m accessible by road from Allos. This northern corner of the park also contains the memorable mountain road over the 2,802m-high Col de la Bonette, which drops down into the Tinée Valley.

However, the Mercantour's acknowledged centrepiece lies further southeast at the Val des Merveilles. The only access to this remote valley is by foot. From St-Dalmas-de-Tende on the N204 north of Saorge (see page 113) the D91 leads west for about 8km to Les Mesches, starting point for a 10km footpath into this dramatic valley with its mysterious Bronze Age rock carvings.

The Mercantour's wildlife could fill a book. More than half of the 4,000 species of wildflowers growing in France are found here, including rare saxifrage, lily and orchid. The park, of course, is the perfect habitat for eagles, buzzards, falcons and kestrels. Other species at home here include chamois, ibex and wild boar.

The Mercantour National Park

RÉSERVE NATURELLE GÉOLOGIQUE DE HAUTE PROVENCE

Eighteen separate sites centred around Digne-les-Bains were declared Nature Reserves in 1984 in an attempt to protect them from damage. The earth's geological record is contained within this spread of valuable sites, which stretches from near Castellane in the south to Barles in the north, a distance of about 50km. They contain deposits of plant life, ammonite skeletons from the time when sea covered the Alps, even traces of bird footprints left some 30 million years ago.

Public access to the sites is controlled. Information on guided visits is available from the Centre de Géologie (open daily) at St-Benoît about 4km from the centre of Digne on the D900. This is a research establishment with exhibition rooms open to the public. It is open 9am–noon, 2–5.30pm (4.30pm on Friday). Tel: 92.31.51.31.

TOURTOUR

Tourtour is typical of the enchanting Provençal villages you invariably stumble across when you wander off the main highways. To find Tourtour, a village in the empty northern spaces of the Haut-Var, take the D77 (off the D557 west of Draguignan), a road that winds up a beautiful wooded escarpment.

The village, a picturesque jumble of vaulted archways, wrought-iron balconies, ancient stone staircases and shadowy passageways – with a fountain at almost every corner – would by now have been buried in souvenir shops were it nearer to the coast. Tourtour's lack of pretension is summed up by the way in which its Post Office is housed in a 16th-century bastion complete with four enormous round corner towers. Although the village show signs of infiltration by craft galleries and expensive eating places, they do not yet dilute a convincingly authentic atmosphere.

From the Église St-Denis, Tourtour's lofty location at over 600m becomes apparent. The church occupies a splendid viewpoint looking southwards to the sea, a panorama fully explained by a helpful *table d'orientation.*

Flowers abound in the pretty and still unspoilt village of Tourtour

LA FRANCE

DIRECTORY

'The resplendent names –
Cannes, Nice, Monte Carlo
– began to glow through
their torpid camouflage,
whispering of old Kings
come here to dine or die ...'
F SCOTT FITZGERALD
Tender Is the Night, 1934

Shopping

*B*est buys in Provence are undoubtedly its local crafts and artefacts. You will not even have to go into a conventional shop for some things. Family potteries, for example, often sell their wares beside the road; sometimes you will find fields the size of football pitches stacked full of kitchenware, urns, plates and pots. At the other end of the spectrum are expensive craft shops and galleries. Some villages, especially the 'perched villages' in southern Provence, have been completely taken over by such shops.

Items on sale include the miniature figures known as *santons* (see page 125), toilette products made from local lavender and herbs, a wide range of pottery, leatherwork, honey, hand-woven baskets and the brightly patterned fabrics of traditional Provençal design. The best – but most expensive – place for the latter is the Souleiado range of stores, located throughout Provence. You can buy the fabric in lengths or already made into dresses, shirts, scarves, tablecloths, etc. Some towns specialise in particular products. Grasse is famous for its perfume, Biot for its exquisite glassware, and Vallauris for its pottery.

Sweets for sale, Aix-en-Provence

WHERE TO SHOP

There seems to be a standard pattern to the larger Provençal towns. The town centre is reserved for the smaller shops, while on the outskirts are sprawling complexes that contain the hypermarkets, motor accessory stores, and the large do-it-yourself and furniture outlets. While the hypermarkets are short on ambience (basically they are huge, functional shopping sheds), they are extremely convenient. In addition to the vast supermarket that forms the core of the centre, you will also find a range of other shops – selling everything from sports goods to musical instruments – all under one roof.

PRICES

Do not try to haggle over prices – bargaining will get you nowhere in Provence. The exception to this rule is the outdoor flea market or antique sale. Here you can often negotiate a reduction of the asking price.

VAT

In certain circumstances visitors to France may have the French value-added tax (VAT) deducted from goods bought in the country. In France VAT is called TVA (*taxe à la valeur ajoutée*), and it goes up to 18.6 per cent or 22 per cent. Visitors from countries outside the EU are exempt from this on purchases above a certain value. In order for residents of the European Union (EU) to claim a duty-free allowance, their purchases from any single store must amount to at least 4,200FF (inclusive of tax) per item; for non-EU residents (but including residents of the Channel Islands and the Isle of Man), the amount is 2,000FF spent at a single store, whatever the number of items. At the time of your purchase, the assistant will give you an 'export sales invoice' (*bordereau* in French), which you must complete to make your claim. Please note that not all shops operate the duty-free sales system.

OPENING HOURS

Shop hours in France respect the sanctity of the midday meal. Apart from the big stores and supermarkets, most shops close between noon and 2pm, though in compensation many stay open until quite late (6 or 7pm). Many towns and villages observe half-day closing at some time during the week. Conventional 'high street' shops are closed on Sunday, though shops aimed at the visitor market – craft shops, galleries, etc – usually remain open, especially in the popular tourist areas.

AIX-EN-PROVENCE
Paul Fouque
This leading maker of *santons* has a shop and workshop.
65 cours Gambetta. Tel: 42.26.33.38.
Souleiado
8 place Chapeliers. Tel: 42.26.23.08.

ARLES
Chrystmar
A gallery of paintings and sculptures.
Place Constantin. Tel: 90.93.78.24.
Souleiado
18 boulevard des Lices. Tel: 90.96.37.55.

AUBAGNE
Poterie Provençal
This pottery is good for straightforward, good-value cookware sold at reasonable prices.
Avenue des Goums. Tel: 42.03.05.59.

AVIGNON
There are many small speciality shops in the maze of narrow streets off the main rue de la République. One of the city's most stylish and exclusive shopping streets is rue Joseph Vernet.

Daniel Robert
You can visit the shop of this painter-sculptor.
Centre Artisanal, rue des Escaliers Ste-Anne. Tel: 90.85.75.25.
Souleiado
5 rue Joseph Vernet. Tel: 90.86.47.67.

Shop sign in Gourdon

BIOT
La Verrière de Biot
Biot's distinctive bubbled glassware is
made and sold here.
Chemin des Combes. Tel: 93.65.03.00.

CANNES
If you must have the latest designer
fashions and expense is no object, then
take your credit cards to the exclusive
boutiques (Chanel, St-Laurent, etc)
along Cannes' La Croisette. Rue
d'Antibes and rue Meynadier are two
more fashionable shopping streets.

EZE
Parfumerie Fragonard
This large perfumery, soap and
cosmetics factory sells its products direct
to the public.
*On the Moyenne Corniche (middle coast
road) between Nice and Monaco.
Tel: 93.41.05.05.*

FONTAINE-DE-VAUCLUSE
Fabrication Artisanale de Papier,
Vallis Clausa
Water-powered machinery helps in the
production of handmade paper, which
is used in a wide range of prints and
maps.
Château de la Fontaine. Tel: 90.20.31.72.

GRASSE
You are spoilt for choice when shopping
for perfume in Grasse – and you should
be able to purchase the perfume at
factory prices. These are a few of the
many outlets in and around the town:
Parfumerie Fragonard
*20 boulevard Fragonard. Tel: 93.36.44.65.
Also 2km from the town centre on the route
de Cannes. Tel: 93.77.94.30.*
Parfumerie Galimard
73 route de Cannes. Tel: 93.09.20.00.

Parfumerie Molinard
*60 boulevard Victor-Hugo.
Tel: 93.36.01.62.*
Le Salon des Parfums
*Parc Industriel Les Bois de Grasse.
Tel: 93.09.00.04.*

MALAUCÈNE
Poterie d'Art Chouvion
Attractive pots, jugs and plates,
predominantly in blue and green, using
local clay and cobalt, copper and iron
oxide for the colours.
Atelier des Isnards. Tel: 90.65.11.74.

MARSEILLE
Santons Marcel Carbonel
This shop and workshop, run by a
famous *santonnier*, also has a small
museum.
*47 rue Neuve Ste-Catherine.
Tel: 91.54.26.58.*
Souleiado
101 rue Paradis. Tel: 91.37.83.16.

MONACO
Matile
This jewellery factory offers guided tours
and an opportunity to purchase items at
discount prices.
8 rue Auréglia. Tel: 93.25.30.05.

NICE
You will find most of the major stores
along avenue Jean-Médecin, the main
shopping thoroughfare, and the more
upmarket Masséna quarter, a
pedestrianised area of chic boutiques.

Confiserie du Vieux Nice
Crystallised fruit is a speciality of Nice.
There are guided tours of this
confectionery, and wide selection of its
colourful range of products.
14 quai Papacino. Tel: 93.55.43.50.

NÎMES
Centre Anglais
An English bookshop for those desperate for a good read.
8 rue Dorée. Tel: 66.21.17.04.

ST-RÉMY-DE-PROVENCE
Les Olivades
The shop specialises in traditional Provençal fabrics – garments and accessories.
28 rue Lafayette. Tel: 90.92.00.80.
Souleiado
2 avenue de la Résistance. Tel: 90.92.45.90.

SALON-DE-PROVENCE
Albert Spinelli
Pottery and ceramics.
168 boulevard David. Tel: 90.56.71.38.
La Maison du Chocolat
A must for chocoholics.
1 rue des Hirondelles. Tel: 90.56.28.38.

SÉGURET
M Fournier
The shop is small – just like the miniature *santons* it sells – but there is a wonderful choice.
Tel: 90.46.91.35.

TOURETTES-SUR-LOUP
Confiserie des Gorges du Loup
Sweet-making is elevated to a fine art at this candied fruit factory and shop.
Le Pont du Loup. Tel: 93.59.32.91.

VALLAURIS
Céramiques N.A.T.O.L.I.
This pottery shop also gives demonstrations in pot-throwing as well as selling its wares.
Avenue Jérôme-Massier/boulevard des deux Vallons. Tel: 93.63.90.14.

Grasse's surrounding meadows yield the flowers for its perfume industry

Markets

*P*rovence's open-air markets are as much a tourist attraction as its beautiful places and historic sites. All the big towns and many villages hold weekly – sometimes daily – markets. The streets are crammed full of stalls, and market-goers shuffle along in the sunshine as the mingling aromas of lavender, herbs, ripe cheese, olives, fresh fish and chicken roasting on a spit waft through the crowds. The markets are the best free show in Provence. Stallholders assail the passing crowds with invitations to sample their wares, and in summer street entertainers soon gather large audiences for impromptu performances of everything from organ grinding to juggling.

You can buy almost anything at a Provençal market. In addition to the cheese, olive, bread, fish, fruit, vegetable, meat and flower stalls, there are large mobile shops that open up to reveal shoes, clothes, toys, hunting gear and gardening equipment. Please note that, in most cases, the markets are mornings only. By noon, the stallholders are beginning to shut up shop and make for home or the nearest café.

AIX-EN-PROVENCE
Daily fruit and vegetable market (place Richelme); flower market on Tuesday, Thursday and Saturday (place de l'Hôtel-de-Ville); fruit, vegetable and herb market on Tuesday, Thursday and Saturday (place des Prêcheurs); antiques market Tuesday, Thursday and Saturday mornings (place de Verdun).

APT
Saturday; pottery market on Tuesday in July and August.

ANTIBES
Daily general market (cours Masséna).

ARLES
Wednesday and Saturday.

AVIGNON
Covered food market Tuesday to Sunday mornings (Les Halles); flea market on Sunday (place des Carmes).

BARJOLS
Tuesday, Thursday and Saturday.

BÉDOIN
Monday.

CANNES
Daily general market (Marché Forville); bric-à-brac market on Saturday (allées de la Liberté).

CARPENTRAS
Friday.

DIGNE
Wednesday, Thursday and Saturday.

DRAGUIGNAN
Wednesday and Saturday;
flea market first Saturday
every month.

FRÉJUS
Wednesday and Saturday.

GORDES
Tuesday arts and crafts
market.

GRASSE
Tuesday.

**L'ÎSLE-SUR-LA-
SORGUE**
Thursday; second-hand,
antiques on Sunday.

JONQUIÈRES
Sunday morning flea
market.

LE LAVANDOU
Thursday.

MANOSQUE
Saturday.

MARSEILLE
Fish market daily except
Sunday (quai des Belges).

MENTON
Daily food market; bric-à-
brac market on Friday.

MONACO
Daily general market (place
d'Armes, Monte-Carlo).

**MOUSTIERS-STE-
MARIE**
Friday.

NICE
Daily market (cours
Saleya) except Sunday
afternoon and Monday;
on Monday, a bric-
à-brac market is held
here.

NÎMES
Monday flower and
antiques market.

ORANGE
Thursday.

**ST-RÉMY-DE-
PROVENCE**
Wednesday and
Saturday.

ST-TROPEZ
Tuesday and Saturday.

**STES-MARIES-DE-
LA-MER**
Monday and Friday.

SALON-DE-PROVENCE
Wednesday.

SANARY-SUR-MER
Wednesday.

SAULT
Wednesday.

SISTERON
Wednesday and Saturday.

TOULON
Daily general market (cours
Lafayette).

VAISON-LA-ROMAINE
Tuesday.

CRAFTS

The variety and quality of craftwork in Provence are evidence of a region in which folk art has achieved a high status. Craft traditions can be traced back at least as far as Roman times, for pottery workshops and kilns of the 1st century AD have been unearthed near Marseille.

POTTERY AND GLASS

The cheapest pottery produced today is called *terre rouge* after the reddish-brown colour it derives from the local red clay. Family workshops turn out jugs, bowls, pots and tiles, which are often sold at the roadside. The more decorative *faïence* style of pottery, first brought to France from Italy in the 16th century, has an enamel porcelain-like finish. Once found only in the homes of the wealthy, its appeal has since broadened considerably. *Grès* pottery, made from the grey clays of central France, lends itself to art pottery because of its hardness.

Another ancient craft has been brought to perfection in the town of Biot, where a unique method is employed to produce swirls of bubbles in clear or coloured blown glass.

PRINTED COTTONS

The vibrant printed cottons of Provence, known as *indiennes* because of their Indian influence, were first produced in the 17th century and have kept their strong appeal over the years. Traditionally they provided the humble shawl for generations of Provençal women, but they have now ventured upmarket and are used for interior decoration, fashion garments and shirts. Their brilliant colours and sharply defined patterns capture the essence of life in this sun-soaked region.

Provençe's crafts are many and varied

Fine pottery, Moustiers ceramics and Gourdon glassware

CONTEMPORARY CRAFTS

The crafts scene in Provence is by no means entirely rooted in traditional folk art. An influx of artists since the 1950s has extended the range of crafts from the earthy to the eclectic, as a visit to almost any gallery will demonstrate. Tradition now coexists with innovation across a whole spectrum of crafts, embracing everything from woven murals to wooden toys.

Entitertainment

*P*rovence is essentially an open-air region. But that doesn't mean dedicated night-clubbers can't find the disco of their dreams. In northern Provence – apart from the main towns and cities – the sleepy, rural economy does not lend itself to frenetic entertainment when the lights go down. By 10pm, this part of Provence is soundly asleep. In the south, of course, it is just the opposite. Along the Riviera, the resorts buzz with life day and night.

CAFÉ SOCIETY

Everybody becomes part of the café society when in Provence. But, like societies the world over, there is a pecking order. You can enjoy a coffee or Coke and watch the world go by in the main square of a humble country town, or pose conspicuously in a celebrated watering place along the coast where the next table just might be occupied by someone famous.

And you will pay for the fame-by-association. Even in ordinary cafés, prices for drinks are high. In the top spots, they are quite outrageous.

AIX-EN-PROVENCE

Cours Mirabeau is the street for pavement cafés and promenading. Les Deux Garçons (53 cours Mirabeau), with its gilt panelling, mirrors and ambience of a more languorous age, attracts an arty crowd.

ARLES

The delightful little square – straight out of Van Gogh – known as the place du Forum is lined with cafés. Bar Le Paris is friendly. There are larger cafés along the boulevard des Lices.

CANNES

You will need a healthy bank balance to enjoy this resort to the full. One of the many attractive spots is the tea room, ice-cream parlour and restaurant of La Grande Brasserie, with its turn-of-the-century décor, at 81 rue d'Antibes.

MONACO

Expect to pay whopping prices anywhere around Monte Carlo's place du Casino, the meeting place of the high-rollers. Prices are a little more sensible – but only just – in the old town of Monaco-Ville across the harbour.

ST-TROPEZ

The cafés along the harbourside quai Jean-Jaurès are the places from which to see it all – the yachts, the parading crowds, the ostentatious displays of wealth.

Charles Garnier re-built the superb casino at Monte Carlo

CASINOS

Unsuccessful gamblers can blame it all on Monte Carlo, for it was here, in 1865, that the Riviera's first casino opened. To add insult to injury, some casinos now impose an admission charge – so you have to pay in order to lose money! Many casinos restrict entry to those 21 and over.

AIX-EN-PROVENCE
Casino Municipal
14 avenue des Belges. Tel: 42.26.30.33.

ANTIBES
La Siesta
Route du Bord de la Mer – direction Nice. Tel: 93.33.31.31.

CANNES
Carlton Casino Club
58 boulevard La Croisette. Tel: 93.68.00.33.
Casino Croisette
Jetée Albert-Edouard/La Croisette. Tel: 93.38.12.11.
Grand Casino Riviera (Noga Hilton)
50 boulevard La Croisette. Tel: 93.68.43.43.

CASSIS
Casino Municipal
Avenue Docteur-Leriche. Tel: 42.01.78.32.

JUAN-LES-PINS
Eden Casino
Boulevard Baudoin. Tel: 92.93.71.71.

MENTON
Casino de Menton
Avenue Félix-Fauré/Promenade du Soleil. Tel: 92.10.16.16.

MONACO
Casino de Monte-Carlo
Place du Casino. Tel: 93.50.69.31.
Loews Casino
Loews Hotel, avenue des Spélugues. Tel: 93.50.65.00.

NICE
Casino Ruhl
1 promenade des Anglais. Tel: 93.87.95.87.

ST-RAPHAËL
Grand Casino
Square de Gand. Tel: 94.95.01.56.

DISCOS, CLUBS, BARS

Elegant piano bars, sophisticated night clubs, raucous discos – you name it and you'll find it, especially along the Riviera. By their very nature, night-time venues tend to come and go as fashions change. Listed here are some of the well-known establishments.

AIX-EN-PROVENCE
Le Scat Club
Rue de la Verrerie. Tel: 42.23.00.23.

ANTIBES
La Siesta
Route du Bord de Mer – direction Nice. Tel: 93.33.31.31.
Shock
Avenue du 11 novembre. Tel: 93.33.69.93.

ARLES
Le Plantation
On the N570 on the outskirts of Arles. Tel: 90.97.11.26.

CANNES
Galaxy
Casino, Jetée Albert-Edouard/La Croisette. Tel: 93.39.01.01.
Whisky à Go-go
115 avenue des Lérins. Tel: 93.43.20.63.

JUAN-LES-PINS
Voom-Voom
1 boulevard de la Pinède. Tel: 93.61.18.71.
Whisky à Go-go
La Pinède. Tel: 93.61.26.40.

MONACO
Tiffany's
Avenue des Spélugues. Tel: 93.50.53.13.

NICE
Le Capitole
2 rue de la Tour. Tel: 93.13.44.33.
Jok Club
Casino Ruhl, 1 promenade des Anglais. Tel: 93.87.95.87.
Le Relais American Bar
Hôtel Negresco, 37 promenade des Anglais. Tel: 93.88.39.51.

ST-TROPEZ
Le Bal
Résidence du Nouveau-Port. Tel: 94.97.14.70.
Les Caves du Roy
Hôtel le Byblos. Tel: 94.97.00.44.

THEATRES

A wide range of concerts, from opera to pop, takes place in many different styles of venue throughout Provence. Some of the most atmospheric performances are held in the open air of a summer's night in Provence's Roman amphitheatres.

AIX-EN-PROVENCE
Théâtre Archevêché
Place de l'Ancien Archevêché.

Toulon's opera house, with its beautifully decorated interior inspired by Charles Garnier

Tel: 42.17.34.00.

Théâtre Municipal
Rue de l'Opéra. Tel: 42.38.44.71 or 42.38.07.39.

ARLES
Théâtre Antique
Rue de la Calade/rue du Cloître. Tel: 90.18.41.20.

MARSEILLE
Opéra Municipal
1 place Reyer. Tel: 91.55.14.99.

MONACO
Opéra de Monte Carlo
The opera house is part of the casino building.
Place du Casino. Tel: 93.50.76.54 for ticket information.
Théâtre Fort Antoine
Avenue de la Quarantaine. Tel: 93.15.88.00.

NICE
Acropolis
Palais des Congrès, Esplanade. Tel: 93.92.80.80.
Opéra de Nice
4 rue St-François-de-Paul. Tel: 93.85.67.31.
Théâtre Municipal du Vieux Nice
4 rue St-Joseph. Tel: 93.62.00.03.
Théâtre de Nice
Promenade des Arts. Tel: 93.13.08.88.

NÎMES
Théâtre Antique
Boulevard des Arènes. Tel: 66.76.72.77.

ORANGE
Théâtre Antique
Place des Frères-Mounet. Tel: 90.51.89.58 for summer night performances.

ST-TROPEZ
Salle de la Renaissance
Place des Lices. Tel: 94.97.48.16.

Festivals

*F*estivals and *fêtes* are a way of life in Provence. They range from small, informal village gatherings to prestigious international events, and embrace all aspects of life. There are festivals that celebrate lavender and lemons, cinema and theatre, religion and the rice harvest, opera and jazz, wine and food. The simple village festivals are great fun. Locals dress up in traditional costume, and there is usually an epic communal meal of many courses and different wines, which anyone can take part in for the price of an all-inclusive ticket. Ask at local tourist offices for details of these. The following list includes most of the major festivals in Provence. Discounting the hype of the Cannes Film Festival (which is not, in any case, aimed at the general public), the main event of the year is Avignon's eclectic summer Festival of Dramatic Art. Aix-en-Provence's Festival of Art and Music is also particularly important.

THE GYPSY FESTIVAL

On 24 and 25 May each year, gypsies from all over Europe make their pilgrimage to Stes-Maries-de-le-Mer, a custom that dates back at least to the 16th century. Their pilgrimage hinges on the figures of Sarah and the three Marys – Mary Magdalen, Mary Salomé (the mother of two Apostles) and Mary Jacobé (Jesus's aunt). According to legend, most of this group settled at Stes-Maries after arriving by boat from the Holy Land. The gypsies adopted the group's servant, Sarah, as their patron saint. On the 24th they carry a black statue of Sarah into the sea to be blessed along with the Camargue and its people, followed by the statues of Mary Salomé and Mary Jacobé on the 25th. In addition to its religious content, the festival is an animated, colourful occasion, with much music, spectacle and dance. A smaller pilgrimage, without the gypsies, takes place in late October

JANUARY
Arles
International Gathering of *Santonniers*.
Tel: 90.96.29.35.

FEBRUARY
Menton
International Lemon Festival.
Tel: 93.57.57.00.
Nice
Carnival and Battle of Flowers.
Tel: 93.87.16.28.

APRIL
Monaco
Monte Carlo Spring Arts Festival (runs until May). *Tel: 93.15.83.03.*

MAY
Cannes
International Film Festival.
Tel: 93.39.01.01.
Stes-Maries-de-la-Mer
24–25: Gypsy pilgrimage.
Tel: 90.97.82.55.
Toulon
Festival of Music. *Tel: 94.93.52.84.*

JUNE
Manosque
Festival of Jazz. *Tel: 92.87.34.41.*
Tarascon
Tarasque Festival. *Tel: 90.91.03.52.*

Celebrating Mardi Gras in Nice

JULY

Aix-en-Provence
Festival of Art and Music.
Tel: 42.17.34.00.
Festival of Dance. *Tel: 42.63.06.75.*
Antibes
Jazz Festival. *Tel: 93.33.95.64.*
Avignon
Festival of Dramatic Art (runs until
August and includes theatre, dance,
music, film and fringe events).
Tel: 90.82.65.11 or 90.82.67.08.
Bormes-les-Mimosas
Festival of Music. *Tel: 94.71.15.08.*
Carpentras
Festival Passion (runs until August and
includes music, dance and theatre).
Tel: 90.63.46.35.
La Ciotat
Festival of Cinema. *Tel: 42.08.88.00.*
Hyères
Festival of Jazz. *Tel: 94.58.44.27.*
L'Îsle-sur-la-Sorgue
Folk Festival. *Tel: 90.38.07.45.*
Orange
Chorégies d'Orange (festival of opera
and classical music). *Tel: 90.34.70.88 or
90.51.83.33.*

St-Rémy-de-Provence
Organa Festival (organ music).
Tel: 90.92.05.22.
Salon-de-Provence
Festival of Jazz. *Tel: 90.56.27.60.*
Vaison-la-Romaine
Festival of Music, Theatre and Dance
(runs until August). *Tel: 90.36.02.11.*

AUGUST

Châteauneuf-du-Pape
First weekend in August: Fête de la
Véraison (marks the change in the colour
of the grape from green to red).
Tel: 90.83.71.08. or 90.83.77.81.
Malaucène
Summer Festival at the beginning of
August. *Tel: 90.65.20.17.*

SEPTEMBER

Arles
Festival of the Rice Harvest.
Tel: 90.96.29.35.
Cassis
Festival of Wine. *Tel: 42.01.71.17.*

NOVEMBER

Marseille
Santons Fair (runs until January).
Tel: 91.54.91.11.

Children

*L*ong-suffering children deserve a break from Provence's Roman remains and medieval sites sometime during the holiday. Attractions range from aquaparks to zoos.

ANTIBES
Marineland

Large attraction with aquariums, displays illustrating the sealife of the Mediterranean, video films, etc. The highlight of the visit is provided by the performing dolphins and killer whales. Other attractions grouped in the same location include an aqua-splash, butterfly jungle, farm park and adventure golf.
RN7-Antibes. Tel: 93.33.49.49. Open: daily throughout the year. Located just off RN7 3km east of Antibes and 12km west of Nice.

AVIGNON
Le Parc du Soleil et du Cosmos

The park takes as its theme the discovery of the universe. Stars and planets speak directly to you (in French) in an imaginatively presented and educational attraction. 'An illustrated alphabet of space.'
Avenue Charles-de-Gaulle, 30133 Les Angles, Avignon. Tel: 90.25.66.82. Open: April to September, daily except Tuesday; otherwise on weekend afternoons only. Closed: mid-December to mid-January.

LA BARBEN
Château de la Barben

Fully furnished château and beautiful gardens standing in 40 hectares of grounds with a large zoo – elephants, lions and other big cats, rhinos, snakes, crocodiles, birds, etc.
13330 La Barben. Tel: 90.55.19.12. Open: 10am–noon, 2–7pm (ticket office closed weekdays in winter noon–1.30pm). Located near Pélissanne just east of Salon-de-Provence.

BEDARRIDES
Oxygène Aquarium Tropical

Three hundred kinds of tropical fish are displayed in this aquarium. You can even walk through a fascinating underwater 'tunnel'.
30 petite route de Sorgues, 84370 Bedarrides. Tel: 90.33.06.87. Open: Tuesday to Sunday 10am–noon, 2–7.30pm. Located between Orange and Avignon.

Children boating in Monte Carlo

BRIGNOLES
Parc Mini-France
France in miniature: mini-mountains, lakes, rivers, plants and trees, together with a play area (full-sized!).
83170 Brignoles. Tel: 94.69.26.00. Open: summer 8.30am–midnight, winter 10am–dusk. Located on RN7 between Marseille and Fréjus.

CHÂTEAUNEUF-LES-MARTIGUES
El Dorado City
Wild West town with daily shows. Cowboy spectacles with stunt men and actors, train rides, puppet theatre and adventure playground. Picnic in the pine forest.
Châteauneuf-les-Martigues. Tel: 42.79.86.90. Open: June to mid-September from 11am. Limited opening mid-March to May and mid-September to mid-November. North of Carry-le-Rouet, which is 25km west of the centre of Marseille.

CUGES-LES-PINS
OK Corral
Themed Wild West funfair. Rides include the Indian Canoe, the Rising Sun and Mountains of the Grand Canyon. Live entertainment, including shoot-outs between cowboys and Indians.
13780 Cuges-les-Pins. Tel: 42.73.80.05. Open: April to September from 10am. Limited opening in October. Located on the RN8 between Marseille and Toulon.

FRÉJUS
Parc Zoologique Safari de Fréjus
You can explore this 20-hectare zoo on foot or by car.
Le Capitou, 83600 Fréjus. Tel: 94.40.70.65. Open: daily throughout the year, May to September, 9.30am–6pm; October to April, 10am–5.30pm..

NICE
Parc des Miniatures
The history of the Côte d'Azur is presented in miniature. Hundreds of models depict scenes and characters from olden days.
Boulevard Impératrice-Eugénie, 06200 Nice. Tel: 93.44.67.74. Open: 9.30am–sunset throughout the year.

Le Parc Phoenix
This wonderland of nature will appeal to all ages – the largest plant house in the world, an Astronomical Garden, Island of Remote Times, Maya Temple, fish, birds, exotic butterflies, thousands of flowers, exhibitions, events and entertainments.
405 promenade des Anglais. Tel: 93.18.03.33. Open: Tuesday to Sunday 10am–sunset throughout the year.

ST-CANNAT
Le Village des Automates
Theme park with animated scenes and puppets: Pinocchio, Gulliver's Travels, Merlin, the circus, etc.
13760 St-Cannat. Tel: 42.57.30.30. Open: April to September, 10am–6pm; October to March, Wednesday, Saturday and Sunday 10am–6pm. Located between Salon-de-Provence and Aix-en-Provence.

SEPTÈMES-LES-VALLONS
Aquacity
Huge aquapark with an amazing variety of slides: free-fall shute, white-water river, cascade, water bobsleigh.
BP 23, 13240 Septèmes-les-Vallons. Tel: 91.96.00.11. Open: June to September from 10am. Located off A51 autoroute between Marseille and Aix-en-Provence.

Sport

*T*he Provençals are no different from the rest of us in their passion for *le foot* (football), motor racing, tennis, golf and water sports. What sets them apart is their love of *boules*, cycling and bullfighting. Any gravelly patch of land is likely to be commandeered as a *boules* pitch for a game that seems like an impromptu version of bowls. Nowhere near as incomprehensible as cricket or American football, it is a restful game to watch, drink in hand, from the comfort of a pavement café.

Cycling is a serious, and strenuous, business in Provence. The steeper the hill, the greater the challenge – and that is quite apart from the heat. The classic cycle climb is the ascent of Mont Ventoux (a regular leg of the Tour de France), an energy-sapping grind of around 20km to an altitude of nearly 2,000m. The Provençal predilection for bullfighting is concentrated in the south, around the Camargue. Animal-lovers can at least rejoice in the fact the bull survives in the Provençal version.

BULLFIGHTING

Bulls come off rather better in Provence than in Spain. The usual spectacle involves the bullfighter, or *razeteurs*, in unfixing a cockade attached to the bull's horns without hurting the animal. But before you attend a bullfight, make sure that it is not the Spanish-style *mise-à-mort* encounter.

The *arènes* (Roman amphitheatres) at Arles and Nîmes are leading venues for bullfighting (Arles tel: 90.96.03.70; Nîmes tel: 66.76.72.77).

CYCLING

Not all of Provence is for macho, masochistic cyclists. Bring your own bicycle, or hire one locally, and enjoy the flattish lands along the Rhône Valley or the Camargue. Along the coast in summer, the sheer volume of traffic can make cycling unpleasant, though you'll at least have the last laugh when it comes to parking.

GOLF

The France Golf International Club has been founded to promote the sport. All member courses must abide by certain standards and rules, and must be open to all players. In Provence, participating clubs include:

Golf des Baux
Mausanne-les-Alpilles, Les Baux-de-Provence. Tel: 90.54.40.20.

Golf de Château-Blanc (Avignon)
Morières-lès-Avignon. Tel: 90.33.39.08.

Golf de Digne-les-Bains
Tel: 92.32.38.38.

Golf de Roquebrune (near Fréjus)
Roquebrune-St-Argens. Tel: 94.82.92.91.

Golf de la Ste-Baume (inland from La Ciotat)
Tel: 94.78.60.12.

Rivera Golf Club de Mandelieu (near Cannes)
Tel: 92.97.67.67.

Other golf courses are also open to visitors. For full details, please write to:

Fédération Française de Golf
69 avenue Victor-Hugo, F–75783 Paris Cedex.

France Golf International
2 rue Linois, F–75740 Paris Cedex.

MOTOR RACING

Monaco is the spiritual home of Formula One Grand Prix racing. Although the narrow street circuit is totally unsuited to today's racing cars (overtaking is virtually impossible), the Grand Prix, held in May, is still the race of the season. During Grand Prix weekend, the cars are not the only things to change gear. Prices in Monaco, never modest at the best of times, shift up another cog in response to the glamour-seeking jet setters and the captive audience of genuine fans.

The South of France's other main motor racing venue is the Circuit Paul Ricard, Route Nationale 8, Le castellet, 83330 Le Beausset. Tel: 94.90.74.90.

RIDING

Horse riding and trekking are widely available in certain parts of Provence. The Camargue, in particular, has many riding centres, which offer anything from a few hours in the saddle to a full day's trekking. All equestrian activities in relation to tourism in France come under the umbrella of the centralised DNTE – Délégation Nationale au Tourisme Équestre de la Fédération Française d'Équitation. More than 1,200 equestrian centres are listed by DNTE. Details from: *Île St-Germain, 170 quai de Stalingrad, 92130 Issy-les-Moulineaux. Tel: (1) 46.48.83.93.*

Practising for the *corrida* (bullfight) in Arles' Arènes (amphitheatre)

SKIING

Inhabitants of the Côte d'Azur live in privileged surroundings. In winter it is quite possible to water-ski along a sunny seashore in the morning and ski on snow in the afternoon. Three major ski resorts lie within a few hours' drive of Nice: Auron, Isola 2000 and Valberg. Despite their southern latitude, they boast excellent snow records.

A little further north, in the Alpes-de-Haute-Provence, the two major ski resorts are Pra-Loup and Super-Sauze near Barcelonnette.

Auron

Range: 1,600m–2,500m with 120km of piste.
Office de Tourisme, 06660 St-Étienne-de-Tinée. Tel: 93.23.02.66.

Isola 2000

Range: 1,800m–2,600m with 112km of piste.
Office de Tourisme, 06420 Isola. Tel: 93.23.15.15.

Pra-Loup

Range: 1,500m–2,500m with 160km of piste.
Office de Tourisme, Maison de Pra-Loup, 04400 Pra-Loup. Tel: 92.84.10.04.

Super-Sauze

Range: 1,400m–2,400m with pistes to suit all skiing abilities.
Office de Tourisme, Immeuble Le Perce-Neige, 04400 Le Sauze/Super-Sauze. Tel: 92.81.05.61.

Valberg

Range: 1,600m–2,450m with 80km of piste and 50km of cross-country ski trails.
Office de Tourisme, 06470 Valberg. Tel: 93.02.52.54.

There are a number of other, smaller ski resorts and stations in Provence, including:
L'Audibergue, Beuil-les-Launes, Le Boréon, La Colmiane-Valdeblore, Esteng-d'Entraunes, Jausiers-la-Frache, La Foux-d'Allos, La Gordoloasque-Belvédère, Gréolières-Les-Neiges, Montagne de Lure, Mont Ventoux, Peira-Cava, Roubion-les-Buisses, St-Auban, St-Dalmas-le-Selvage, Ste-Anne-la-Condamine, St-Jean-Montclar, Tende-Caramagne, Turini-Camp-d'Argent and Val-Pelens-St-Martin-d'Entraunes.

A selection of 01891 snow information telephone numbers operates within the UK. Some of the resorts mentioned here are part of the Ski France service. For further information, please contact: 61 boulevard Haussmann, 75008 Paris. Tel: (1) 47.42.23.32; snow bulletin (1) 42.66.64.28.

WALKING AND CLIMBING

Walking and hiking are extremely well-organised in France. A network of long-distance footpaths and trails covers the whole of the country, from north to south, east to west. These marked paths are known as 'GRs' (*Sentiers des Grandes Randonnées*), each of which bears an identifying number like a road or motorway.

Some of the most popular walking areas in Provence are the Lubéron Hills, Massif des Maures and Mont Ventoux. These areas offer hilly terrain and – in the case of the Maures and Ventoux – a good covering of cool, green forest.

The mountains of the Alpes-de-Haute-Provence and Alpes-Maritimes provide a much more serious challenge. Walkers can spend days and weeks in this dramatic landscape – the higher parts of which

The beach resort of Bandol Bay is ideal for windsurfers

remain snow-covered throughout the year – stopping overnight in remote hostels or mountain huts.

Rock climbing is a major activity in the mountains. All levels of difficulty can be tackled. Experienced climbers are particularly attracted to the Parc National du Mercantour (see page 139), where the ascents range from difficult to very difficult.

June to October is the best time to enjoy the high mountains. Keep a watch out for the weather – it can change very quickly. And always be well prepared.

Walking Information
Centre d'Information Sentiers et Randonnées
64 rue Gergovie, 75014 Paris.
Tel: (1) 45.45.31.02.

Fédération Française de la Randonnées Pédestres
8 avenue Marceau, 75008 Paris.
Tel: (1) 47.23.62.32.

Climbing Information
Club Alpin Français
24 avenue Laumière, 75019 Paris.
Tel: (1) 42.02.75.94.

Fédération Française de la Montagne et de l'Escalade
16 rue L-Dardenne, 92170 Vanves.
Tel: (1) 41.08.00.00.

WATER SPORTS

Although conditions in the placid Mediterranean are not perfect for serious sailing and windsurfing, this does not seem to put many people off. There are marinas and harbours packed with expensive yachts all along the coast. Windsurfers can easily hire equipment at many of the local beaches and sports shops.

Diving conditions are good, though marine life has suffered along the Riviera through overfishing and pollution. Away from the coast, Provence's lakes and rivers provide excellent water sports opportunities.

Further information is available from these national organisations:
Canoeing/Rafting
Fédération Française de Canoë-Kayak
87 quai de la Marne, 94340 Joinville-le-Pont. *Tel: 48.89.39.89.*

Diving
Fédération Française d'Études et des Sports Sous-Marins
24 quai de Rive-Neuve, 13007 Marseille.
Tel: 91.33.99.31.

Water-skiing
Fédération Française de Ski Nautique
16 rue Clément-Marot, 75008 Paris.
Tel: (1) 47.20.05.00.

OLIVES

The black cypress and the silvery olive tree dominate large parts of the Provençal landscape. The mournful beauty of the cypress has inspired many a poet; the olive, a tough evergreen, serves a more practical purpose. Originally imported from Greece, it has long had a vital role in the agrarian economy of Provence.

THE HARDY OLIVE

One of the principal virtues of the olive, for the canny farmers of Provence, is that it thrives in barren areas, taking root in poor, rocky soil and surviving great heat and aridity. What is more, it is long-lived: many of the groves climbing the hillsides have been tended by succeeding generations of farmers. The trees grow to a height of around 7.5m and often achieve impressive girth. Its handsome hard wood is sometimes carved into kitchen utensils and other objects.

As anyone who has visited a Provençal market will confirm, olives are taken very seriously in this part of France. For a start, there are stalls dedicated to the sale of olives and nothing else; and you are not – heaven forbid! – given a choice of merely black or green, but myriad variations on a theme, all laid out in open containers for tasting beforehand. There are olives with garlic, olives with peppers and olives with herbs, bitter and smooth-tasting olives – even plain black and green olives.

OIL AND COSMETICS

Then there are the bottles of olive oil, a staple ingredient of Provençal culinary art. The extraction of oil from the ripened fruit is a comparatively simple process, and over the years the oil press has been as widely used in Provence as the wine press.

Nyons – centre of
olive production

The olives, black
when ripe, are first
pressed to a pasty
consistency, then put
in woollen bags and
subjected to
considerable pressure.
The resulting product
is considered the finest
of vegetable oils, and is
used not only in food
preparation but in fine
soaps and cosmetics.

Food and Drink

*P*rovence, like the rest of France, reveres its food. Meals are anything but a means to an end. They rise above mere sustenance into occasions with aesthetic and social dimensions – which explains why meals are never hurried, there are deliberate pauses between courses, and everything still stops for lunch.

You will always find exceptions to these generalisations, but they will be confined to the larger towns and cities where the universal fast-food mentality is making its presence felt. In small-town Provence and in the country areas, traditional values still apply. But do not set your expectations too high. While many French restaurants serve food that is streets ahead of their counterparts in other countries, there are others – an increasing number – that seem content to live on past reputations and play down to the tourist trade. Ask the locals – they will always know the best places to eat.

Restaurants range from the very expensive (usually along the coast) to the amazingly cheap. Go for the fixed-price menu of three or four courses, with limited choice per course. Many restaurants offer a few versions of these, ranging from the basic *menu touristique* (which usually features chicken, trout, steak and chips, etc) to the elaborate *menu gastronomique* with regional specialities.

Bread (a cut-up *baguette*) is always provided, along with water. House wine is usually quite inexpensive, though some of the classier bottles can be surprisingly dear in comparison to their supermarket price.

For those with a small appetite, many cafés and bars serve snacks and light meals. Cafés will also serve breakfast – a large cup of milky coffee, bread, jam and sometimes *croissants*.

Along with wine, the staple drink of Provence is *pastis*, a strong aniseed-flavoured aperitif served with ice and water (see page 170–1). Locals swear that they can tell the difference between the main brands, Pernod, Ricard and Pastis. Beer is served by the bottle or, in most cafés, on draught as *bière pression*, the cheaper option.

Soft drinks include *orange pressé* (freshly squeezed orange juice), *citron* (lemon) *pressé*, and fizzy Orangina. There is a wide choice of mineral waters including the famous Perrier, which is bottled locally in the west of the Rhône delta. Only ask for *café* if you like your coffee served black at paint-stripping strength. Most visitors prefer the *café crème* or *café au lait* version served with milk.

Prices

The listing that follows is a selection of places to eat across a wide price range. The following symbols have been used to indicate the average cost per person of a three-course meal, not including drink. All taxes and service charges are usually included in the price.

le cabanon du chinois

DÉPOT de PAIN

Antibes has a wide range of eating places to choose from

F = under 100 francs
FF = under 150 francs
FFF = under 200 francs
FFFF = over 200 francs

WHERE TO EAT
AIX-EN-PROVENCE
Le Clos de la Violette FFFF
One of the top restaurants in Aix, which serves innovative and traditional cuisine. For best value, eat here at lunchtime on weekdays.
10 avenue de la Violette. Tel: 42.23.30.71.

ANTIBES
La Bonne Auberge FFFF
A famous Riviera restaurant with a warm ambience and exceptional modern cuisine – and prices to match.
Quartier de la Brague – the N7 coast road just over 4km from Antibes. Tel: 93.33.36.65.

Restaurant du Bacon FFFF
The place to go – outside Marseille – for the traditional fish stew called *bouillabaisse*. Otherwise, try one of the many other delicious seafood dishes on offer.
Boulevard du Bacon, Cap d'Antibes. Tel: 93.61.50.02.

ARLES
La Côte d'Adam F
Small, friendly and excellent value. The restaurant's fixed-price menus have a creative touch, with interesting combinations and sauces. Just off the popular place du Forum.
12 rue de la Liberté. Tel: 90.49.62.29.

Le Vaccarès FFF/FFFF
Innovative Provençal dishes, based on meats and seafood, are served in this elegant restaurant.
9 rue Favorin, place du Forum. Tel: 90.96.06.17.

AVIGNON
La Fourchette FF
Good-value bistro with local specialities.
17 rue Racine. Tel: 90.85.20.93.

Hiély-Lucullus FFFF
A charming restaurant with a formidable reputation. One of Provence's gastronomic shrines.
5 rue de la République. Tel: 90.86.17.07.

LES BAUX-DE-PROVENCE
Auberge de la Benvengudo FFFF
Although in the top price category
(everything in Les Baux is expensive!),
your bill at this attractive, informal inn
will be considerably cheaper than in
L'Ousteaù de Baumanière (see next
entry).
*Vallon de l'Arcoule, route d'Arles.
Tel: 90.54.32.54.*

L'Ousteaù de Baumanière FFFF
This is the place to go for a once-in-the-
holiday – or maybe a lifetime –
indulgent gastronomic experience. The
atmosphere is formal and reserved.
Expect a *big* bill – it is way off the
humble price scale.
Le Vallon. Tel: 90.54.33.07.

CAIRANNE
Auberge Castel Mireio F/FF
An elegantly appointed restaurant in the
heart of Côtes-du-Rhône wine country.
Good service and food.
Route d'Orange. Tel: 90.30.82.20.

CANNES
Au Bec Fin F/FF
Excellent-value fixed-price menus at
this cheerful family-run bistro near the
train station. The *salad niçoise* is
especially good.
12 rue du 24-Août. Tel: 93.38.35.86.

La Mère Besson FFFF
A favourite Cannes restaurant serving
authentically prepared traditional
specialities.
*13 rue des Frères-Pradignac. Tel:
93.39.59.24.*

La Pizza F/FF
The name says it all!
3 quai St-Pierre. Tel: 93.39.22.56.

Villa Dionysos FF/FFFF
Well-thought-out menus covering a wide
price range. The outstanding Italianate
décor is as much a talking point as the
food.
7 rue Marceau. Tel: 93.38.79.73.

CASSIS
Chez Vincent F/FF
Simple restaurant on the port with the
emphasis on fish and *bouillabaisse* (fish
stew).
Quai des Baux. Tel: 42.01.35.19.

GORDES
La Mayanelle FFF/FFFF
The cuisine is inspired by traditional
and regional influences – you will enjoy
good, honest Provençal flavours. As a
bonus, there are beautiful views across
to the Lubéron Hills from the outside
terrace.
6 rue Combe. Tel: 90.72.00.28.

MARSEILLE
La Flamiche F/FF
Seafood restaurant that offers excellent
value.
16 rue de la Paix. Tel: 91.33.00.74.

MONACO
Le Café de Paris FFF/FFFF
You do not have to spend a fortune here
to enjoy a reasonable meal. International
dishes are served in glittering *belle époque-*
style surroundings.
Place du Casino. Tel: 93.50.57.75.

Le Louis XV FFFF
The most elegant restaurant in Monaco,
part of the Hôtel de Paris. Outstanding
cuisine served in a formal atmosphere.
Very expensive but you might well find
yourself seated next to royalty.
Place du Casino. Tel: 92.16.30.01.

MOUGINS
Le Feu Follet FF/FFF
Exclusive Mougins has a reputation for
sky-high prices. Yet this restaurant
manages to offer quality cuisine at
sensible rates.
Place de la Mairie. Tel: 93.90.15.78.

NICE
L'Ane Rouge FFFF
Small, but with a huge reputation as
Nice's best seafood restaurant. Located
on the harbour.
*7 quai des Deux-Emmanuel. Tel:
93.89.49.63.*

Restaurant l'Estocaficada F/FF
Down-to-earth local restaurant
specialising in seafood.
2 rue de l'Hôtel-de-Ville. Tel: 93.80.21.64.

ORANGE
Le Parvis FF/FFF
Fresh local products, traditional cooking
with an original touch, and well-priced
menus explain this restaurant's
popularity.
3 cours Pourtoules. Tel: 90.34.82.00.

STE-CÉCILE-LES-VIGNES
L'Angelus F
Amazingly good value at this welcoming
pizzeria/restaurant. Try the pizza or the
spaghetti, washed down by a bottle of the
excellent local Côtes-du-Rhône.
27 cours du Portalet. Tel: 90.30.73.70.

ST-RÉMY-DE-PROVENCE
La France F
Patriotically named restaurant with
hearty local food and inexpensive fixed-
price menu.
2 avenue Fauconnet. Tel: 90.92.11.56.

Eating out at Le Beffroi in Vaison-la-Romaine

ST-TROPEZ
Bistrot des Lices FFFF
Glamorous bistro that attracts the
celebrities.
3 place des Lices. Tel: 94.97.29.00.

Le Girelier FFF
Reasonably priced (for St-Tropez) fish
restaurant located on the quay. Go for
the fixed-price menu.
Quai Jean-Jaurès. Tel: 94.97.03.87.

VAISON-LA-ROMAINE
Le Beffroi FF/FFF
Go here for the setting alone. The
restaurant is part of a 16th-century hotel
idyllically situated high in the medieval
town. The food is good too!
*Rue de l'Évêché, Haute Ville. Tel:
90.36.04.71.*

PROVENÇAL CUISINE

In classic Provençal cuisine, freshness
and inherent flavour are everything.
Provençals leave the rich, creamy sauces
to their northern countryfolk, preferring
instead to let the ingredients speak for
themselves. Although garlic is liberally
used, it tends to be milder in the South
of France than in the north. Garlic is a
mainstay of the distinctive Provençal
cuisine, along with olive oil, herbs like
basil, rosemary and thyme, and the
tomato, or *pomme d'amour* (love apple).
If you have been brought up on the
bland shrink-wrapped supermarket
version of the tomato, then fear not: the
plump, tasty Provençal variety is similar
only in colour.

Harvest of the sea

The Provençals are justly proud of their
fish dishes such as *soupe de poisson*, a
work of art taking hours to prepare. A
variation on this theme is the famous

bouillabaisse, a speciality of the Marseille
coast. *Bouillabaisse* is not really a soup at
all. The fish are served on a side dish,
while the garlic- and saffron-flavoured
stew in which they were cooked comes

separately so that diners can dunk their bread into it. Another classic dish is *bourride*, a white fish stew served with *aïoli*, a rich mayonnaise of garlic and olive oil known as 'the butter of Provence'.

Meat, cheese and fruit

Lamb also figures prominently in the local cuisine. The spicy *agneau de Sisteron* comes from the mountain pastures of Provence, while the lambs grazing on the salt marshes of the coast provide *agneau de pré-salé*. *Boeuf à la gardianne* is a popular beef stew cooked with red wine, vegetables, black olives and herbs. Another speciality of the region is *farci* (stuffed vegetable). Onions are stuffed with garlic, cabbages with parsley and sausage.

Cheeses, which are served before the dessert, include the local *banon*, wrapped in vine or chestnut leaves, and the peppery *poivre d'âne*. Fruit is plentiful – and be sure to make the most of the mouthwatering melons, best bought in quantity from local markets when they are just beginning to split.

Eating out in Provence is a delight, and the food seems to taste even better when you dine *al fresco* on a terrace shaded by parasols or vines. Lunch is served early, from about 12 noon, with dinner from 7 to 7.30pm. Fast food is an anathema to the Provençals, and so is fast service. You are meant to take your time, for each course is served to be savoured, not rushed. *Bon appétit!*

WINES AND SPIRITS

Drinking a glass or two of a chewy, deeply textured Côtes-du-Rhône Village – a Cairanne perhaps, or a Gigondas, Rasteau or Vacqueyras – on the terrace on a warm summer's evening is one of the great pleasures of Provence. And it is a pleasure made even more satisfying in the knowledge that this full-bodied red wine, bought direct from the local vineyard, has cost little more than the standard supermarket plonk back home.

THE REDS OF THE RHÔNE

Parts of Provence are almost entirely dedicated to the production of wine: drive along the flanks of the Rhône Valley around Orange and Avignon, and you will see regimented rows of vines stretching into the distance. These vineyards yield the robust, peppery generic Côtes-du-Rhône and the even better versions named after individual villages or growers.

The top wine from the region is Châteauneuf-du-Pape, a full, rich red with a perfumed raspberry bouquet, which often does not peak until a decade or so after bottling.

Although its reds reign supreme (a consequence of the hot climate), Provence produces wines to suit all occasions. In addition to the deep – and highly alcoholic – reds, there are delicate rosés and dry and sweet whites. Tavel and Lirac rosés are both exceptionally good. Beaumes-de-Venise is mostly famous for its thick, sweet wine made from the muscat grape and served chilled as an apéritif or dessert wine (a similar wine is also produced in Rasteau).

The wines from the coastal strip around Bandol – reds, rosés and whites – have a character all their own, while the whites of nearby Cassis are fresh and aromatic.

Other, less well-known wine-producing areas in Provence include Côtes-du-Ventoux, Côtes-du-Lubéron, Côtes-de-Provence and Côteaux d'Aix.

The region's vineyards produce some of France's most famous red wines

STRONG STUFF

Pay attention to the alcoholic content of Provençal wines. It tends to be higher – in some cases, substantially so – than the usual 10 to 12 degrees. The same word of warning applies to *pastis*, the traditional aniseed-flavoured spirit drink of Provence. Normally over 50 degrees proof (though you can purchase weaker versions), it is served as a long drink, and the spirit turns milky when ice and water are added.

Hotels and Accommodation

For families and couples, hotels in France usually offer good value because you pay by the room, not per person. Along the Riviera, this money-saving arrangement is undermined by high room rates; in rural Provence, though, you will usually be pleasantly surprised by the accommodation you can purchase for relatively modest sums.

Many visitors to Provence – especially families or large groups of friends – prefer to self-cater. Along the coast, and in the hills just inland, there is a large choice of apartments and luxury villas. Summer rates for the sought-after properties are high. For better value, go further inland – which, in any case, is the true Provence – and rent a more modest country property.

Camping, of course, is the ultimate budget alternative. The French are a nation of ardent campers, so you can expect to find an excellent choice of well-organised sites with comprehensive facilities.

For business travellers

The main commercial centres of Cannes, Marseille, Monaco and Nice have many three- and four-star hotels geared to the business traveller and conference delegate. Cannes, for example, has the Noga Hilton (5 boulevard de la Croisette, tel: 92.99.70.00; fax: 92.99.70.11), while at Nice there is the Holiday Inn (20 boulevard Victor-Hugo, tel: 93.16.55.00; fax: 93.16.55.55).

The French Hoteliers Association operates a handy advance reservations system. If a member hotel is fully booked, it will offer an alternative where available, or suggest another suitable location. Stays of one or more nights are accepted. Members with hotels in key business locations in Provence include:

Alliance (tel: 0181–392 1838; fax: 0181–392 1318); Concorde (tel: 0171–630 1704; fax: 0171–630 0391); Mercure (tel: 0181–741 4655; fax: 0181–748 3542); and Méridien (tel: 0171–439 1244; fax: 0171–439 1230).

HOTELS

Hotels in France are classified by the Ministry of Tourism under the following categories:

Four Star L = luxury
Four Star = deluxe
Three Star = first class
Two Star = tourist class, good quality
One Star = budget

For overnight accommodation you usually pay by the room (based on a twin/double); breakfast is extra. Half-board rates are normally available for longer stays. Most hotels quote rates that include service and tax.

HOTEL CHAINS

France has many hotel groups and associations. The largest cover the entire country, though some are confined to a particular region. The accommodation ranges from purpose-built places (such as Formule 1), which offer a no-frills budget overnight stay, to beautifully converted country properties rich in atmosphere and charm.

Here is a selection of some of the leading groups:

Châteaux et Hôtels Indépendants

There is a good selection of these characterful hotels around the Rhône Valley and along the coast between St-Tropez and Nice.

15 rue Malebranche, 75005 Paris.
Tel: (1) 43.54.74.99.

Climat de France

A chain of modern two-star hotels and restaurants; well-represented in Provence.

BP 93, 91943 Les Ulis Cedex.
Tel: (1) 64.46.01.23.

Formule 1

Convenient and cheap overnight accommodation located at roadsides throughout France.

Immeuble le Descartes, 29 promenade Michel-Simon, 93163 Noisy-le-Grand.
Tel: (1) 43.04.01.00.

Logis de France

There are over 4,500 members of this well-known group, which sets out to offer straightforward yet comfortable accommodation, good hospitality and service, and good regional cooking.

83 avenue d'Italie, 75013 Paris.
Tel: (1) 45.84.70.00.

Relais et Châteaux

A well-established group of historic buildings – former castles, abbeys, manor houses, etc – converted into luxurious inns and hotels.

9 avenue Marceau, 75116 Paris.
Tel: (1) 47.23.41.42.

Le Relais du Silence

Hotels renowned for their quiet charm and peaceful surroundings.

2 passage du Guesclin, 75015 Paris.
Tel: (1) 45.66.77.77.

THE LAP OF LUXURY
Some of the stylish hotels in the South of France are favoured by the expense-is-no-object business traveller – and anyone else who can afford the glamorous life. Two such places are the famous Carlton Inter-Continental in Cannes (58 La Croisette, tel: 93.68.91.68; fax: 93.38.20.90) and the equally celebrated Negresco in Nice (37 promenade des Anglais, tel: 93.88.39.51; fax: 93.88.35.68). In Monaco the last word in luxury is offered by the Hôtel de Paris (place du Casino, tel: 92.16.30.00; fax: 93.25.59.17).

BED AND BREAKFAST

The nearest equivalent to the British B&B is the Gîtes-Chambres d'Hôtes, usually situated in farmhouses or villages and ranging in size from one to several bedrooms.

La Maison des Gîtes de France, 35 rue Godot-de-Mauroy, 75439 Paris Cedex 09. Tel: (1) 47.42.25.43.

SELF-CATERING

The Gîtes Rural de France are holiday homes, usually in country or village locations, that offer accommodation across four different grades. Although they have a rustic image, some *gîtes* – especially those in the top categories – can provide comfortable and charming accommodation, and might even have a private swimming pool. In Provence, *gîtes* are in great demand, so if you want the peak summer months, book early.

See 'Bed and Breakfast' for address details.

There are many companies that specialise in letting private houses and villas. Ask your travel agent for details, or look out for the newspaper adverts.

CAMPING

Campsites range from the deliberately basic in the hills and mountains – for those who want to savour the natural environment – to the big family complexes inland and along the coast with swimming pools, restaurants and central facilities. The French are passionate – and extremely professional – campers, so you can expect the big sites to have the full range of amenities, including swimming pools, shops and family recreation facilities. Some also have permanently sited, fully furnished mobile homes for six to eight people; travel agents can advise you of firms that specialise in mobile homes, as well as large pre-erected furnished tents, on quality campsites.

At the other end of the scale there are simple sites – usually in rural locations – with basic facilities. The best overnight rates are to be found at municipal

Balcony of Hôtel Isenard – Grasse

campsites (*camping municipal*) run by local authorities. Camping *à la ferme* (on the farm) is also good value for money. Expect to pay hefty premiums for camping along the Côte d'Azur. For full details on campsites, contact the French Tourist Office's Maison de la France, 178 Piccadilly, London W1V 0AL; tel: 0891–244123.

Fédération Française de Camping et de Caravanning
78 rue de Rivoli, 75004 Paris. Tel: (1) 42.72.84.08.

YOUTH ACCOMMODATION
Auberges de Jeunesse (Youth Hostels) are a good budget option, particularly for single travellers (if you are travelling as a couple or in groups, cheap hotels – where you pay by the room – will usually be just as good value). To take advantage of hostel accommodation, join the International Youth Hostel Federation through YHA, Trevelyan House, St Stephen's Hill, St Albans AL1 2DY (tel: 0727-855215). You can also join at most French hostels. If you want a little more luxury, then try the Foyers des Jeunes Travailleurs. Available in some of the larger towns, these hostels provide comfortable, low-priced accommodation for students and young workers.

HOW TO BOOK
For more details, contact the French Government Tourist Office (see **Tourist Offices**, pages 189). The office in your country may well produce specialist books on *gîtes*, for example. You will also find it worthwhile to contact direct the *département(s)* of Provence in which you are interested (again, see address details under 'Tourist Offices'). They should be able to send you detailed lists of hotels, *gîtes*, campsites, etc for their area.

Campsite at Castellane

On Business

*C*oastal Provence is nowadays as much a business destination as a place for holidays and leisure. Indeed, the balance has swung in favour of the business traveller in places like Nice and Cannes, which now rely more on conventions, exhibitions and meetings than on their pleasure-seeking clientele of old.

Business delegates are big spenders; on average, their daily expenditure amounts to anything between 1,500 and 2,000 francs per person. The French Business Travel Club (Club Français du Tourisme d'Affaires Réceptif, or CFTAR) has been established to service and encourage this trade. This government-approved organisation brings together more than 120 members representing all facets of business travel – convention facilities, accommodation, ground handling, study tours, seminars, transportation, etc. For further information, contact the French Government Tourist Office in your country (see Tourist Offices, pages 189 for address details).

THE BIG THREE

Cannes, Monaco and Nice are the three destinations that attract most of the Côte d'Azur's business and conference trade. All three have major modern convention centres in imposing – and stunning – locations that reflect their pre-eminence within the local economy.

CANNES

Palais des Festivals et des Congrès (Cannes Conference Centre)

A vast modern building overlooking the harbour, with the full back-up of the latest technology and multi-use adaptable floor space.

La Croisette, 06400 Cannes. Business and group travel tel: 93.30.01.01; fax: 93.99.37.34.

Also contact:

LSO International

Conference and convention organiser, product launches, special events.

23-25 boulevard Général-Vautrin, 06400 Cannes. Tel: 93.94.16.00; fax: 93.43.40.02.

MONACO

Centre de Congrès Auditorium (Monte Carlo Convention Centre and Auditorium)

This is part of a boldly designed complex of buildings fronting the sea below the casino. The hexagonal structure is on four levels, with the full complement of ultra-modern facilities.

Boulevard Louis II, Monte Carlo, 98030 Monaco. Tel: 93.50.93.00.

Centre de Rencontres Internationales (International Conference Centre)

Located above the harbour, this facility complements the Centre de Congrès Auditorium.

12 avenue d'Ostende, Monte Carlo. Tel: 93.50.34.44.

Further enquiries concerning business and conference matters (including more details on the above centres) should be addressed to the following offices:

Monaco

Direction du Tourisme et des Congrès

de la Principauté de Monaco, *2a boulevard des Moulins, Monte Carlo, MC 98030 Monaco Cedex. Tel: 92.16.61.66.*

UK

Monaco Government Tourist and Convention Office, *3–18 Chelsea Garden Market, Chelsea Harbour, London SW10 0XE. Tel: 0171-352 9962; fax: 0171-352 2103.*

USA

Monaco Government Tourist and Convention Bureau Offices at:
845 Third Avenue, New York, NY 10022. Tel: (212) 759-5227; fax: (212) 754-9320.
542 South Dearborn Street, Suite 550, Chicago, IL 60605. Tel: (312) 939-7863; fax: (312) 939-8727.
101 Center, Suite 4E, La Jolla, CA 92037. Tel and fax: (619) 459-8912.

NICE

Acropolis (Nice Conference Centre)
This centre offers the ultimate in business communications and support facilities. It is set in magnificent gardens decorated with fountains and sculptures by famous artists.
1 esplanade Kennedy, 06302 Nice Cedex 4. Tel: 93.92.83.00; fax: 93.92.82.55.

Also contact:
Nice Convention Bureau
Based at the Acropolis. Tel: 93.92.80.70/93.92.80.71; fax: 93.92.80.85.

FLYING IN

The success the Riviera enjoys as a business and conference centre is in no small measure due to the existence of Nice–Côte d'Azur International Airport, only 8km from the centre of Nice. The airport daily handles over 90 direct flights from 34 countries. Terminal 1 is for international and domestic flights; Terminal 2 is for domestic flights only.

In the arrivals area you will find the 2A Services (short for Accueil Affaires Services), which is run by the Chamber of Commerce and Industry. It provides multi-lingual hostesses who can arrange whatever you need to carry out your business – secretarial services, temporary office accommodation, meeting rooms, computer, fax and modem facilities. *Airport tel: 93.21.30.30.*

FURTHER INFORMATION

Useful information is available from the Economist Intelligence Unit. This publishes quarterly reports on France as well as an annual country profile, which contain essential business information. *Economist Intelligence Unit, Publications Department, 40 Duke Street, London W1A 3DW. Tel: 0171-830 1000.*

The Department of Trade and Industry also publishes a country profile on France. The DTI may be able to assist with market research costs (up to 50 per cent) if you intend doing business in France, and organises the representation of British firms at trade fairs in Nice and elsewhere.
Department of Trade and Industry, Business in Europe Branch, 66–74 Victoria Street, London SW1E 6SW. Tel: 0171-215 4765/5197.

You may also find it helpful to make individual contact with Provence's departmental Chambres de Commerce et d'Industrie. Details from:
French Chamber of Commerce, 2nd Floor, Knightsbridge House, 197 Knightsbridge, London SW7 1RB. Tel: 0171-225 5250.

Practical Guide

ARRIVING

By car

Many visitors choose to drive to Provence. The most popular cross-Channel route (and underwater link, with the opening of *Le Shuttle*) is Dover to Calais.

From Calais, the autoroute runs all the way to Provence. Although the tolls are expensive, the autoroute is the fastest option – with the caveat that it becomes exceedingly congested and accident-prone during the busy weekends in July and August, when all of France seems to be heading south along the *Autoroute du Soleil* (the A6 from Paris, which becomes the A7 at Lyon).

The best autoroute from Calais is not the A1 to Paris, which plunges you into the confusion of the notorious *périphérique* ring road around the capital, but the A26/A5/A31 via Reims, joining the A6 just south of Dijon. This route – which, as well as avoiding Paris, cuts out large stretches of the busy A6 – can be surprisingly quiet. The A6 south from Dijon has recently been improved with the opening of the loop around Lyon, avoiding a nasty bottleneck.

Motorists sailing to Le Havre can also avoid Paris by travelling cross-country to Chartres and picking up the A71 to Clermont-Ferrand, joining the A7 just south of Lyon.

If you prefer to drive at a more leisurely pace, taking a few days to reach Provence, there is an excellent toll-free system of well-maintained and marked N (national) and D (departmental) roads. As you pass through towns, villages and beautiful countryside on these less-travelled routes, you get a real taste of the country as a whole and the changing character of the land as you journey southwards.

By train

The easiest but most expensive car journey of all is the motorail option. SNCF (French Railways) runs a motorail service from Calais to Avignon, Fréjus/St-Raphaël and Nice; also from Paris to the same destinations plus Marseille and Toulon. Telephone 0171-409 3518, or call in at French Railways' London office (see below).

Rail travellers can take advantage of SNCF's excellent TGV (*Train à Grande Vitesse*) high-speed service from Paris (only 3 hours 45 minutes to Avignon and 4 hours 40 minutes to Marseille). A range of discounted tickets is available, giving unlimited travel on the French and other European rail networks. For details call in at the Rail Shop, French Railways, 179 Piccadilly, London W1V 0BA. Or telephone 01891–515477 for train information or 01345–300003 for bookings.

The *Thomas Cook European Timetable* will help you plan a rail journey to, from and around France. It gives up-to-date details of most rail services and many shipping services throughout Europe. It is available in the UK from some stations, any branch of Thomas Cook, or by telephoning 01733–268943. In the USA, contact the Forsyth Travel Library Inc, 9154 West 57th Street (PO Box 2975), Shawnee Mission, Kansas 66201. Tel: 0800–367-7982 (toll-free).

By coach

The services operated by National Express Eurolines are a budget alternative to rail travel. Coaches operate direct on three main routes, all starting from London's Victoria Coach Station: to Avignon and Nîmes (four times a week in summer, weekly in winter); to Aix-en-Provence, Marseille and Toulon, with a twice-weekly extension in summer to Hyères, Fréjus and St-Raphaël (twice a week in summer, weekly in winter); and Sisteron, Grasse, Cannes, Juan-les-Pins and Nice (twice a week in summer). Passengers travel on the same coach throughout, so there is no tiresome unloading of luggage for the cross-Channel journey. Journey times are surprisingly good (just over 18 hours London to Avignon, for example).

For further details telephone 01582–404511. Booking office and further details are also available at National Express Eurolines, 52 Grosvenor Gardens, Victoria, London SW1W 0AU; tel: 0171–730 8235.

Nice airport

By air

Provence is well served by scheduled flights to a number of airports: Nice–Côte d'Azur (tel: 93.21.30.30), Marseille–Provence (tel: 42.78.21.00) and Lyon–Satolas (tel: 72.22.72.21). Although the latter is not in the region, good autoroute links make it a more convenient gateway than Nice for parts of northern Provence.

Air France and British Airways operate a comprehensive range of services. Air UK operates a daily summer service from London (Stansted) to Nice, and British Midland flies daily from London (Heathrow) to Nice.

CAMPING
See page 174.

CHILDREN
See pages 156–7.

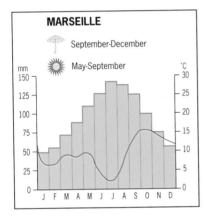

MARSEILLE

September-December

May-September

CLIMATE
Provence, which consists of high
mountains as well as a Mediterranean
coastline, has some regional variations
in its climate; for example, the ferocious
wind known as the *mistral* (see pages
12–13) affects mainly the Rhône Valley.
Nevertheless, it is safe to say that,
overall, Provence is a sunny place. Along
the Côte d'Azur there are 2,500 to 2,800
hours of sunshine per year.

June and September are the best
months to travel. The weather is
pleasantly hot (and can remain so into
October), the days are long, and there
are no summer crowds. It can become
very hot in July and August, especially
away from sea breezes.

It does not rain very often in
Provence – but when it does, it pours.
Late August can bring tremendous
thunderstorms and torrential downpours.
Average rainfall, though, is low, less than
800mm a year. If Provence has a rainy
season, then it is in November and
December.

CONVERSION TABLES
See tables opposite.

CRIME
Provence is not immune to the growing
problem of car theft. It is particularly rife
in the Camargue and some of the main
cities. So be careful where you park your
car, and make sure that all valuables are
locked away safely out of sight. Similarly,
try not to stand out in a crowd – tourists
are perceived as soft targets by thieves.
Wear a moneybelt, or keep your bag
strapped across your body. If you are
robbed, contact the police immediately
and get a signed note for your insurance
claim (*déclaration de perte*).
See also **Emergencies**.

CUSTOMS REGULATIONS
Those allowed to enter France without a
visa (for stays of up to 90 days) include
citizens from EU countries, the USA,
Canada and New Zealand. All categories
of travellers, except holders of a National
Identity Card, must be in possession of a
valid passport. For full details, please
check with the nearest French Consulate.

Travellers from Australia and South
Africa will need a visa. People requiring
visas should get them in their country of
residence, as it may prove difficult to get
them elsewhere. In the UK, the Thomas
Cook Passport and Visa Service can
advise on and obtain the necessary
documentation.

Men's Suits

UK		36	38	40	42	44	46	48
Rest of Europe	46	48	50	52	54	56	58
US		36	38	40	42	44	46	48

Dress Sizes

UK		8	10	12	14	16	18
France		36	38	40	42	44	46
Italy		38	40	42	44	46	48
Rest of Europe		34	36	38	40	42	44
US		6	8	10	12	14	16

Men's Shirts

UK	14	14.5	15	15.5	16	16.5	17
Rest of Europe	36	37	38	39/40	41	42	43
US	14	14.5	15	15.5	16	16.5	17

Men's Shoes

UK		7	7.5	8.5		9.5	10.5	11
Rest of Europe	41	42	43		44		45	46
US		8	8.5	9.5	10.5	11.5	12

Women's Shoes

UK		4.5	5	5.5	6	6.5	7
Rest of Europe	38	38	39	39		40	41
US		6	6.5	7	7.5		8	8.5

Conversion Table

FROM	TO	MULTIPLY BY
Inches	Centimetres	2.54
Feet	Metres	0.3048
Yards	Metres	0.9144
Miles	Kilometres	1.6090
Acres	Hectares	0.4047
Gallons	Litres	4.5460
Ounces	Grams	28.35
Pounds	Grams	453.6
Pounds	Kilograms	0.4536
Tons	Tonnes	1.0160

To convert back, for example from centimetres to inches, divide by the number in the the third column.

DISABLED TRAVELLERS

In recent times, more efforts have been made to welcome travellers with disabilities. In addition to providing better on-the-ground facilities, individual resorts and areas produce publications that give information on accommodation, transport, recreational activities, access to historic monuments, museums, theatres, etc.

For more information, contact: Association des Paralysés, Délégation de Paris, 17 boulevard Auguste-Blanqui, 75013 Paris. Tel: (1) 40.78.69.00.

Comité National Français de Liaison pour la Réadaptation des Handicapés (CNFLRH), Point Handicap, 38 boulevard Raspail, 75007 Paris. Tel: (1) 45.48.98.90.

In Britain, contact: Maison de la France, 178 Piccadilly, London W1V 0AL. Tel: 01891–244123.

A fact sheet on France is available from the Holiday Care Service, 2 Old Bank Chambers, Station Road, Horley, Surrey RH6 9HW. Tel: 01293–774535. The *AA Guide for the Disabled Traveller* is another helpful publication.

DRIVING

In France, of course, you drive on the right. As far as driving habits are concerned, although generalisation is always a tricky business, it is fair to say that the French tend to drive faster – and are more impetuous and short-tempered – than the British or the Americans. Cross-country routes are sometimes blissfully traffic free, though towns and cities can be intimidating at times. (A useful strategy for getting through towns is to make for the town centre, or *centre-ville*, then look out for signs indicating the way out of town in your preferred direction.)

Accidents

If no policeman is around, note the number of the other vehicle involved, lock your car and go with the driver of the other vehicle in search of a policeman. The policeman will make out a report in triplicate, noting all the relevant facts. Try to obtain names and addresses of witnesses. Send the report to your insurance company. If the accident is serious, it is a good idea to take photographs.

Breakdowns

If your car does not have hazard warning lights, you must carry a warning triangle, which you should place 30m behind your car in the event of a breakdown (it is useful to have one anyway, in case the breakdown affects your lights). You must carry a set of spare headlight bulbs. On autoroutes there are emergency telephones every 2km.

Car hire

To hire a car in France, drivers must have been in possession of a valid driving licence for at least one year. The minimum age is 21, though some companies insist on 25.

Car rental is easily available throughout Provence, but it is more expensive than in most other European countries. Ask at your travel agent for details of fly-drive holidays; it is usually much cheaper to book your car and flight this way than to make separate arrangements.

All the major car hire companies are represented at airports and cities in Provence – Hertz, Avis, etc. If you make your reservation before your departure, you may be able to take advantage of discounts or special rates. Take heed: the most expensive way to hire a car is to turn up at an airport desk without having made any prior arrangements.

One company that offers particularly good rates, usually below those of the major operators, is Holiday Autos, 25 Savile Row, Mayfair, London W1X 1AA; tel: 0171–491 1111.

Chauffeur-driven cars

Every chauffeur-driven limousine company in France should have an administrative licence issued by the Ministry of Tourism (a *grande remise*) or by the *Préfectures* in each *département* (a *petite remise*). Around a hundred companies have the Ministry of Tourism licence. Most are affiliated to the national association of chauffeur-driven car companies:
Chambre Syndicale Nationale des Entreprises de Remise et de Tourisme, 48 rue de la Bienfaisance, 75008 Paris. Tel: (1) 45.62.06.66.
If you have a car available and you want to hire a chauffeur, contact:
Société de Chauffeurs, 132 rue d'Assas, 75006 Paris. Tel: (1) 46.34.77.07.

Documents

The minimum age for driving is 18. You will need to bring your driving licence, the vehicle registration document and insurance certificate. Although a Green Card – which gives you comprehensive cover and is available from your insurance company – is no longer required by law, it is strongly recommended.

Petrol

Please bear in mind that in some of Provence's remoter hill and country areas, petrol stations can be few and far between – and may well be closed altogether on Sundays. Look out for cheaper prices at larger supermarkets and hypermarkets.

Rules of the road

The *priorité à droite* (priority to the right) rule still causes confusion. Outside built-up areas, traffic flowing on the main route usually has the right of way at junctions and crossroads, which are normally signposted with a cross saying *Passage Protégé*. Within built-up areas, vehicles coming from the right – even on the most minor roads – still have priority. In practice, the French seem as confused as the rest of us over the interpretation of this arcane rule – so be extra vigilant at junctions and, if in doubt, give way.

In recent years, the French have discovered the value of roundabouts – new ones are cropping up all over the country. Thankfully, an unambiguous rule applies: you must give way to vehicles already on the roundabout, as instructed by the sign *Vous n'avez pas la priorité* (you do not have priority).

In addition to a warning triangle and headlight bulbs (see **Breakdowns**), your car should have a national identity sticker and be fitted with headlight beam deflectors. Under-10s should travel in the rear seats, and the wearing of all seat belts fitted in the car is compulsory.

Speed limits

Speeds in brackets relate to adverse weather conditions (eg heavy rain, fog, ice). Toll motorways 130kph/80mph (110kph/68mph). Non-toll motorways and dual carriageways 110kph/68mph (100kph/62mph). Other roads 90kph/55mph (80kph/50mph). Towns and built-up areas 50kph/31mph.

Please note:
Rappel means the continuation of a restriction or of a previously signposted speed limit.

The minimum speed for the outside lane of a motorway during daylight on level ground with good visibility is 80kph/50mph.

ELECTRICITY

The supply is 220 volts using Continental two-pin round plugs. You will need an adaptor if you are taking your own appliances.

EMBASSIES AND CONSULATES

Australia

4 rue Jean-Rey, 75724 Paris, Cedex 15. Tel: (1) 40.59.33.00.

Canada

35 avenue Montaigne, 75008 Paris. Tel: (1) 47.23.01.01.

Ireland

12 avenue Foch, 75116 Paris. Tel: (1) 45.00.20.87.

New Zealand

7 rue Léonard-da-Vinci, 75016 Paris. Tel: (1) 45.00.24.11.

UK

35 rue du Faubourg St-Honoré, 75383
Paris, Cedex 08, and its consular section
at 16 rue d'Anjou, 75008 Paris. Tel: (1)
42.66.38.10. Also at 24 avenue du
Prado, 13006 Marseille. Tel: 91.53.43.32.

USA

2 avenue Gabriel, 75382 Paris, Cedex
08. Tel: (1) 42.96.12.02/42.61.80.75.
Also at 12 boulevard Paul-Peytral, 13286
Marseille. Tel: 91.54.92.00.

EMERGENCIES

The Thomas Cook Worldwide Customer
Promise offers free emergency assistance
at any Thomas Cook network location to
travellers who have purchased their travel
tickets at a Thomas Cook location. In
addition, any MasterCard cardholder
may use any Thomas Cook Network
location to report loss or theft of their
card and obtain an emergency card
replacement as a free service under the
Thomas Cook MasterCard International
Alliance. Thomas Cook travellers'
cheque refund is a 24-hour service.
Report loss or theft within 24 hours, tel:
05.90.83.30 (toll-free).

Emergency telephone numbers

Ambulance: 15
Fire: 18
Police: 17

HEALTH

There are no mandatory vaccination
requirements, and no vaccination
recommendations other than to keep
tetanus and polio immunisation up to
date. As in every other part of the world,
AIDS is present. It is quite safe to drink
the tap water served in hotels and
restaurants, but never drink from a tap
labelled *eau non potable* (not drinking
water).

Up-to-date health advice can be
obtained from your Thomas Cook travel
consultant or direct from the Thomas
Cook Travel Clinic, 45 Berkeley Street,
London W1A 1EB (tel: 0171–408
4157). This is open for consultation
without appointment Monday to Friday,
8.30am–5.30pm, and can give
vaccinations as well as supply medical
advice and a range of first-aid and travel
health items.

HITCH-HIKING

In Provence, unlike other parts of
France, hitch-hiking is quite common.
The usual common-sense provisos apply.
Do not hitch-hike alone, and be wary of
isolated spots. Hitch-hiking is not
allowed on autoroutes.

HOTELS

Travellers who purchase their travel
tickets from a Thomas Cook network
location are entitled to use the services of
other Thomas Cook network locations,
free of charge, to make hotel
reservations.

INSURANCE

All EU countries have reciprocal
arrangements for reclaiming the cost of
medical services. UK residents should
obtain forms CM1 and E111 from their
post office. These provide detailed
information on what is covered and how
to claim. Claiming is often a long drawn-
out process, and you are only covered
for medical care, not for emergency
repatriation, holiday cancellation and so
on. You are strongly advised to take out
a travel insurance policy. You can
purchase such insurance through the AA,
branches of Thomas Cook and most
travel agents. For motor insurance
advice, see **Documents** on page 183.

LANGUAGE

Even if you speak only a little French, the effort will be appreciated. English is widely spoken on the coast, much less so in rural Provence. But whatever your location, you will find that your efforts to speak French, however limited, are appreciated.

Monday *lundi*
Tuesday *mardi*
Wednesday *mercredi*
Thursday *jeudi*
Friday *vendredi*
Saturday *samedi*
Sunday *dimanche*

0 *zéro*	8 *huit*	16 *seize*	30 *trente*	100 *cent*
1 *un, une*	9 *neuf*	17 *dix-sept*	40 *quarante*	200 *deux cents*
2 *deux*	10 *dix*	18 *dix-huit*	50 *cinquante*	300 *trois cents*
3 *trois*	11 *onze*	19 *dix-neuf*	60 *soixante*	
4 *quatre*	12 *douze*	20 *vingt*	70 *soixante-dix*	1,000 *mille*
5 *cinq*	13 *treize*	21 *vingt et un*	80 *quatre-vingts*	2,000 *deux mille*
6 *six*	14 *quatorze*	22 *vingt-deux*	90 *quatre-vingt-dix*	1,000,000 *un million*
7 *sept*	15 *quinze*			

yes *oui*
no *non*
please *si'l vous plaît*
(any request or enquiry should be accompanied by this phrase)
thank you *merci*
good day *bonjour*
good morning
(when addressing anyone in this way, it is common courtesy to add *monsieur* for a man, *madame* for a woman or *mademoiselle* for a girl or young woman)
good evening *bonsoir*
goodbye *au revoir*
yesterday *hier*
today *aujourd'hui*
tomorrow *demain*
the morning *le matin*
afternoon *l'après-midi*
the evening *le soir*
man *un homme*
woman *une femme*
big *grand*
small *petit*

a lot *beaucoup*
a little *un peu*
open *ouvert*
closed *fermé*
hot *chaud*
cold *froid*
car *voiture*
railway station *gare*
bus station *gare routière*
bakery *boulangerie*
supermarket *supermarché*
bank *banque*
toilets *toilettes*
post office *PTT, poste*
stamps *timbres*
chemist *pharmacie*
hospital *hôpital*
petrol *essence*
airline *ligne à air*
Do you speak English? *Parlez-vous anglais?*
I do not understand *Je ne comprends pas*

OK/agreed *D'accord*
Where? *Où?*
How much?/ How many? *Combien?*
Excuse me *Pardon*
Have you a room? *Avez-vous une chambre*
Have you a room with a private bath? *Avez-vous une chambre avec bain?*
How much does it cost? *Combien ça coûte?*
I feel ill *Je suis malade*
Have you a double room? *Avez-vous une chambre à deux lits?*

LOST PROPERTY

Report loss of valuables to the police and get a copy of the statement for making an insurance claim. Cancel lost credit cards and travellers' cheques immediately. A lost passport should be reported at once to your nearest embassy or consulate.

MAPS

A wide range of maps is available (for the best prices try some of the larger supermarkets, which have good guide-book/map sections). Most tourist offices will have free town maps.

MEDIA

In the major towns and cities, English-language newspapers are widely available. *Le Monde* is a respected national daily newspaper. Better for listings and local events are regional newspapers such as *La Marseillaise*, the leftist *Le Provençal* and the right-wing *Le Méridional*. Along the Côte d'Azur you will be able to pick up the English-language Radio Riviera.

MONEY MATTERS

The unit of currency is the French *franc*, which is equal to 100 *centimes*. Bank hours vary, but typical times are Monday to Friday, 9am–noon, 2–4pm. All banks are closed on Sunday and public holidays. Some are open on Saturday but closed on Monday.

One of the simplest, cheapest and most secure methods of exchange is the travellers' cheque. Usually it is advantageous to purchase cheques denominated in French francs, as opposed to pounds sterling or dollars. Most banks should then give you the face value of the cheque, without deducting any further charges. Eurocheques, backed up by a card, are also convenient.

Thomas Cook MasterCard travellers' cheques free you from the hazards of carrying large amounts of cash, and in the event of loss or theft can quickly be refunded (see **Emergencies**).

Probably the most cost-effective way of all is payment by credit card; there is no transaction fee and you get the best rate of exchange. The major cards (Visa, MasterCard, etc) are now widely accepted throughout Provence.

OPENING HOURS

Apart from the big cities, France shuts down between noon and 2pm each day. In compensation, shops open very early, and many – especially the smaller stores – do not close until quite late, sometimes 8pm. Many petrol stations and the larger supermarkets remain open throughout the day, especially in summer, as do the main tourist attractions, museums and tourist offices. Normal business hours are 8/9am–noon, and 2–6pm.
See **Money Matters, Pharmacies** and **Post Offices** for further opening details.

PHARMACIES

These are recognised by the sign of a green cross. They give medical advice as well as sell a wide range of products (prescription and non-prescription). Many stock familiar brands of nappies (*couches*), tampons and sanitary towels (*serviettes hygiéniques*), though these can also be bought at supermarkets. Machines dispensing condoms (*préservatifs*) are increasingly being installed outside pharmacies. You will always find an open pharmacy in the area – details are posted on pharmacy doors.

PLACES OF WORSHIP

Every town and village has a Catholic church. There are synagogues in

Avignon, Carpentras and Cavaillon. Local tourist offices have futher details.

POLICE

Country areas and smaller places are covered by the *Gendarmes* police force (blue trousers, black jackets and white belts). In towns and cities, policing is provided by the *Police Municipale* (blue uniforms). The highway police are the *Garde Mobile* or *Police de la Route*. The emergency telephone number is 17. In the case of very serious problems, you should contact your Consulate immediately (see **Embassies and Consulates**).

POST OFFICES

Post offices – known as PTTs or *postes* – are usually open 9am–noon and 2–5pm, though there are many variations (main post offices will open earlier, stay open throughout lunch time, and close later). You can buy stamps or telephone cards here, and some will change Eurocheques. If you just want stamps, you can avoid the inevitable queues by purchasing them at *tabacs* (tobacconists) and some hotels.

You can use post offices to receive mail through the *Poste Restante* system. Letters should be addressed with your surname printed in capital letters and underlined, followed by Post Restante, Poste Centrale, and the postcode and name of the town.

PUBLIC TRANSPORT

Along the main communication corridors in Provence – the north-south Rhône Valley and the east-west Côte d'Azur – rail and bus services are very good. Buses and trains also operate in rural and mountainous Provence, but services are patchy and by no means comprehensive.

In addition to the main rail routes, a line runs up the Durance Valley into the Alps. There are many local bus companies but not much co-ordination of services between them. There are also local buses run by SNCF (French Railways), which serve places on rail routes where trains do not stop (rail tickets and passes are valid on these).

The only feasible way to explore off-the-beaten-track Provence is by car, bicycle or on foot. Local tourist offices and bus stations are good sources of advice and information.

Bus stations: Aix-en-Provence tel: 42.27.17.91; Avignon tel: 90.82.07.35; Marseille tel: 91.08.16.40; Nice: tel: 93.85.61.81.

For details of unlimited-travel rail passes, please contact:

UK
The Rail Shop, French Railways, 179 Piccadilly, London W1V 0BA. Tel: 01891-515477 for train information; tel: 01345–300003 for bookings.

USA
Rail Europe, Inc, 226–230 Westchester Avenue, White Plains, New York 10604. Tel: (800) TGV–RAIL.

SENIOR CITIZENS

Visitors enjoy the same benefits as France's own senior citizens. Reduced admission (usually 50 per cent) is available at most museums. The *Carte Vermeille*, which is sold at railway stations, entitles the holder to reduced fares on public transport.

STUDENT AND YOUTH TRAVEL

More than 25 per cent of visitors to France are young people under the age of 26. A whole range of special services and facilities exists for this influential group.

The *Carte Jeune* (Youth Card) entitles holders – who must be under 26 – to discounts on public transport, museum admissions, entertainments, shopping and other facilities (including meals at university canteens). The card is widely available from many outlets. Ask for details at tourist offices or post offices, or contact:

Centre d'Information et Documentation Jeunesse (National Youth Information and Documentation Centre), 101 quai Branly, 75740 Paris Cedex 15. Tel: (1) 44.49.12.00. For Auberges de Jeunesse (Youth Hostels), see page 175.

There are special rail fares for under-26s on SNCF. Contact the Rail Shop for details (see **Public Transport** for address and telephone numbers).

TELEPHONES

French telephones operate on an eight-figure number without the usual area code. When phoning anywhere in France, simply dial the eight figures, except in the case of Paris. When calling Paris from the provinces, dial 161 before the eight-figure number. From Paris to the provinces, dial 16 first. Within Paris, just dial the eight-figure number.

To make an international call from France, first dial 19 (wait for the new tone), then the national code (44 for the UK, 1 for the US and Canada, 353 for Ireland, 61 for Australia), followed by the area code and number. Please note that you have to omit any initial 0 in the area code (eg, 171 or 181 for London). For international enquiries, dial 19.33.12 plus the country code.

To telephone France from abroad, first dial the correct international code (010 from the UK) followed by 33 (for France) and the eight-figure number.

For Paris, the international code is followed by 331.

The vast majority of telephone boxes in Provence are equipped with the *Télécarte* (phonecard) system, and are not coin-operated. When you insert your card into the phone slot, the remaining amount of credit is displayed, and you can see this amount decreasing as you use the phone. Phonecards can be bought at post offices, tobacconists and newsagents. International calls can be made from any box with the sign of a blue bell.

Cheap rates apply weekdays from 9.30pm to 8am, Saturday after 2pm and all day Sunday. Note that hotels usually make a substantial surcharge for the use of phones in rooms.

TIME

France observes Central European Time. For the UK and Ireland, France is one hour ahead of Greenwich Mean Time from late September to late March, and two hours ahead for the rest of the year. France is six to nine hours ahead of the USA, five to nine hours ahead of Canada, seven to nine hours behind Australia and 11 hours behind New Zealand.

TIPPING

In restaurants and cafés, service is generally included in the bill. If not, leave an extra 10–15 per cent (it is customary to leave some small change even when service is included). Taxi drivers should be tipped 10–15 per cent of the amount on the meter. In hotels, tip porters 5–10 francs for every item of baggage and chambermaids about 10 francs a day. Cloakroom attendants in theatres and restaurants should be tipped about 5 francs per item, toilet attendants

2 francs, usherettes in cinemas and theatres 2 francs, and guides at museums and historic monuments about 5 francs. A 10 per cent tip should be given to hairdressers.

TOILETS

There are public toilets at railway and bus stations, in public buildings and in stores. In the smaller towns, there may be one toilet for both men (*hommes* or *messieurs*) and women (*dames*).

TOURIST OFFICES

For initial information on Provence, contact the French Government Tourist Office in your country.

Australia

BNP Building, 12th Floor, 12 Castlereagh Street, Sydney, NSW 2000. Tel: 02–231 5244.

Canada

Headquarters: 1981 Avenue McGill College, Suite 490, Montréal, QUE H3A 2W9. Tel: (514) 288–4264.
Regional Office: 30 Saint Patrick Street, Suite 700, Toronto ONT M5T 3A3. Tel: (416) 593–4723.

Ireland

35 Lower Abbey Street, Dublin 1. Tel: 1–77 18 71.

UK

Maison de la France, 178 Piccadilly, London W1V 0AL. Tel: 01891–244123 (calls charged at 36p per minute cheap rate, 48p per minute at other times).

USA

Headquarters: 610 Fifth Avenue, Suite 222, New York, NY 10020–2452. Tel: (212) 757–1125.
Midwest: 645 North Michigan Avenue, Chicago, Illinois 60611–2836. Tel: (312) 337–6301.
South: 2305 Cedar Springs Road, Suite

205, Dallas, Texas 75201. Tel: (214) 720–4010.
West Coast: 9454 Wilshire Boulevard, Beverly Hills, Los Angeles, CA 90212–2967. Tel: (310) 271–7838.

Although the first point of contact is your country's French Tourist Office, it is often worth getting in touch directly with the region for the most up-to-date, comprehensive literature (though it will, of course, be largely in French).

Comité Régional de Tourisme, Provence-Alpes-Côte d'Azur, 2 rue Henri-Barbusse, 13241 Marseille Cedex 01. Tel: 91.39.38.00.

Also the following departmental offices:

Alpes-de-Haute Provence

Boulevard Victor-Hugo, BP 170, 04005 Digne Cedex. Tel: 92.31.57.29.

Alpes-Maritimes

55 promenade des Anglais, 06011 Nice. Tel: 93.37.78.78.

Bouches-du-Rhône

6 rue du Jeune-Anacharsis, 13001 Marseille. Tel: 91.54.92.66.

Var

BP 99, 83003 Draguignan Cedex. Tel: 94.68.59.33.
5 avenue Vauban, 83000 Toulon. Tel: 94.09.00.69.

Vaucluse

Place Campana, La Balance, BP 147, 84008 Avignon. Tel: 90.86.43.42.

When in France, use the local network of tourist information offices – the *Office de Tourisme* or *Syndicat d'Initiative* – located in most towns and many villages. In addition to providing details of local events, walks, activities, etc, some will change money and help with accommodation booking for a small fee.

ACKNOWLEDGEMENTS

The Automobile Association wishes to thank the following photographers and libraries for their assistance in the preparation of this book:

COURTAULD INSTITUTE GALLERIES 114a, 114b; MARY EVANS PICTURE LIBRARY 28a, 28b, 107a, 107b, 107c, 115a, 115b, 132c; FOOTPRINTS 20 (N Hanna), 91 (N Hanna); RONALD GRANT ARCHIVES 98, 99b, 106b; NATIONAL GALLERY 56; NATURE PHOTOGRAPHERS LTD 126 (P R Sterry), 127a (K J Carlson), 127c (M E Gore); REX FEATURES LTD 99a, 99c; SPECTRUM COLOUR LIBRARY 13b, 97a, 168b.
The remaining photographs are held in the Automobile Association's own library (AA PHOTO LIBRARY) and were taken by Adrian Baker with the exception of the spine which was taken by P Kenward and pages 19, 95, 110, 111, 116, 120, 122, 124a, 132a, 132b and 139 which were taken by R Moss; page 49 which was taken by T Oliver; cover and pages 63b, 70, 82, 88a, and 146 which were taken by B Smith; inset and pages 4, 7, 8, 13a, 15b, 16, 21, 29a, 29b, 32a, 32b, 33, 34, 40/1, 41b, 42a, 43, 57, 59, 61a, 61b, 62, 63a, 66, 73, 75, 81, 86, 87, 94, 96, 97b, 113, 117a, 117b, 119b, 126/7, 134, 135, 137a, 137b, 141, 142 and 148a which were taken by R Strange.

The author would like to thank Sylvie Keulian of the Comité Régional de Tourisme, Provence-Alpes-Côte d'Azur for her invaluable assistance. Also British Midland Airways, Holiday Autos and France Location Vacances en Résidences for help with travel arrangements. Thanks should also be given to François and Claude Delesse and Roland and Annie Éberlé, friends in the Vaucluse whose unfailing enthusiasm and hospitality make Provence an even more appealing place.

CONTRIBUTORS
Series Adviser: Melissa Shales   **Designer:** Design 23   **Copy Editor:** Janet Tabinski
Verifier: Joanna Whitaker   **Indexer:** Marie Lorimer